NO-BAKE
DESSERTS

Cherry-Cinnamon Crème Anglaise, page 118

NO-BAKE
DESSERTS

RODALE

Cover photograph: Mitch Mandel
Cover recipe: Tiny Fruit Tarts
Courtesy of Nestlé, page 43
Food stylist: Diane Vezza
Illustrations: Judy Newhouse

Editorial produced by:
BETH ALLEN ASSOCIATES, INC.
President/Owner: Beth Allen
Art Production Director: Laura Smyth (smythtype)
Culinary Consultant/Food Editor: Deborah Mintcheff
Recipe Editor: Jackie Mills
Public Relations Consultants: Stephanie Avidon, Melissa Moritz
Nutritionist: Michele C. Fisher, Ph.D., R.D.

Library of Congress Cataloging-in-Publication Data

No-bake desserts.
          p.   cm.
     Includes index.
     ISBN-13 978-1-59486-143-7 hardcover
     ISBN-10 1-59486-143-9 hardcover
     1. Desserts.   2. Quick and easy cookery.   I. Rodale (Firm)
   TX773.N63   2005
   641.8'6—dc22   2004023611

2 4 6 8 10 9 7 5 3 1   hardcover

CONTENTS

INTRODUCTION

Dozens of homemade desserts—without turning on the oven!

Look at the smiles that surround you as you serve that mouthwatering chocolate cream pie. You've probably seen those happy faces before. Like maybe the time you brought strawberry cheesecake to the bake sale and saw someone take that first bite. Or when the kids from your daughter's first-grade class were jumping up and down with joy for the red and white popcorn balls you made for Valentine's Day. All of these sweet moments (and smiles!) are now easier and faster than ever before. Thanks to this collection of 100 *No-Bake Desserts*.

Take a fast peek at the many more happy times you have in store when you serve the fast and easy sweets inside these pages—all without ever turning on your oven. Start off with one of the "Fix 'em Fast!" desserts—they're perfect for any weeknight supper. Stir up an old-fashioned rice pudding the super-quick way (in less than 30 minutes), microwave a batch of No-Bake Fudge Cookies (page 22) in minutes, or double-dip fresh strawberries with two different chocolates (page 20).

Now take a look at the "Fresh Fruit Endings." We have a farmers' market full of fresh fruits—all turned into delicious desserts the no-bake way. Layer fresh berries and ladyfingers into our Raspberry Trifle (page 51), or "wow" your guests some evening by stirring up Bananas Foster (page 39) right at the table.

Since we all know that kids love sweets, we've created a whole collection of recipes just for them—from Snickerdoodle Ice Cream (page 54) to Wake 'em Up Wacky Waffles (page 62) and a fun Circus Pie (page 73), which they can help make. Find out how easy it is to "Chill It!" and serve a spectacular Strawberry Chiffon Pie (page 76) or a Chilled Orange Soufflé (page 82), right out of your fridge. Whirl up some Berry Blender Ice Cream (page 96) in the summertime and serve some old-fashioned Banana Splits (page 99) when the gang drops by after the game. On weekends around the holidays, when the you have a little more time, make the Triple Layer Eggnog Pie (page 138) and serve it proudly . . . it's as easy as pie!

But that's only the beginning of what The Quick Cook series has in store for you. We've teamed up with food professionals, cooking pros, and test kitchens of well-known food manufacturers across the country to collect 100 ways to enjoy dessert, without turning on the oven. Naturally, all the recipes have been tested and retested to ensure success, whether you're a seasoned cook or just learning. Our *On the Menu* feature discusses how folks serve dessert in different regions of the country and even around the globe.

As in our other Quick Cook books, *No-Bake Desserts* is much more than a recipe book. We've tucked in some *Cooking Basics* features that show you the best way to cut up a fresh pineapple and provide the simple 1,2,3's for making crepes (page 136). In our *Cook to Cook* sections, cooks just like you share ways to top ice cream cones (page 97) and how to melt chocolate perfectly smooth without it burning, or seizing (the answer is on page 85).

But that's not all. You'll find that your microwave is indispensable for making many no-bake desserts. There are hot fruit sauces to whip up (page 28) and cool-cook candies to make—all fast and easy by *Microwave in Minutes*. And naturally we've included some useful *Time Savers*, such as how to chill desserts faster and how to make fruit pops quicker (page 57). And when you have a few minutes, check out *Food Facts*—you'll learn all about how the very first ice cream cone came to be (the answer is on page 97).

Start discovering right now how *No-Bake Desserts* can become your new best friend in the kitchen. Turn the page and begin by reading "Desserts in a Dash." You'll find some of the new tools on the market, such as S'mores kits, plus a handy ice cream freezer whose bowl tucks right into your freezer, just waiting to help you freeze homemade ice cream in about 30 minutes, at the touch of a button. Plus, we've included a chart that outlines many different ways to fill an ice cream sandwich and lots of ways to serve cake 'n' cream.

While you're exploring *No-Bake Desserts*, remember that in the near future you'll be able to enjoy many more fabulous time-saving and great-tasting ideas in other books in the collection of The Quick Cook series. Inside each book you'll find exactly what you want in today's cookbooks—quick-cooking recipes, beautiful photographs, and lots of helpful tips. The books are guaranteed to become your valued kitchen advisor, bringing you easy no-bake dessert recipes, news of brand-new kitchen tools, and tried-and-true techniques from corner to corner.

May *No-Bake Desserts* bring your family great-tasting desserts—and give you more smiles than you ever thought possible!

Chocolate Lover's Ice Cream Pie, page 100

Desserts in a Dash

Feeling like something sweet? How about short-cakes filled with fresh fruits, two scoops of home-made sorbet, or a slice of pie—all made the easy no-bake, fast-cook way in almost no time at all? That's what desserts in a dash are all about. Turn the page and discover the latest ingredients that make our collection of no-bake desserts exciting—from lots of different chocolates to whipped cream toppings of many flavors. Then come on a shopping trip for a fast 'n' easy ice cream maker, pop mold, and even a S'mores maker. Back home, try one of the cake 'n' cream creations or ice cream sandwiches for dessert tonight—and wait for the compliments!

Snickerdoodle Ice Cream, page 54

Cherry-Cinnamon Crème Anglaise, page 118

Tropical Cheesecake, page 114

WE ALL SCREAM FOR ICE CREAM!

Ice cream is perhaps the most classic of no-bake desserts. And with good reason. No matter what our age, we never seem to outgrow our love for ice cream. Though just who actually invented this beloved treat remains a mystery. Some historians trace it back to China during the Tang Dynasty around 1,000 C.E., where it was supposedly invented as a special treat for the emperor, perhaps using snow as a base ingredient. Others believe the first flavored ice creams made from whole milk or cream were made in Italy and then in France during the seventeenth century.

Yet ice cream is only one type of popular frozen dessert. Here's some of what you can expect to find these days in your local grocer's frozen food case or specialty shops:

BOMBE An elegant frozen dessert consisting of layers of ice cream, at least two flavors, and sometimes sherbet too. Softened ice cream is spread in a thick layer inside the tall mold and allowed to freeze before another layer is added. After it is frozen solid, it is unmolded. The cut wedges make a dramatic presentation.

COUPE Ice cream or sherbet topped with fruit and whipped cream and glazed chestnuts (marrons glacés).

FRENCH ICE CREAM Begins with a cooked egg custard that is frozen to creamy perfection.

FROZEN YOGURT Made from milk that has been fermented and coagulated due to the presence of "friendly" bacteria. Its texture is similar to soft-serve ice cream.

GELATO The Italian word for ice cream. The Italian version contains less air (and others use butterfat) than American-style ice cream. It can be used interchangeably with ice cream.

ICE CREAM Must contain at least 10% milk fat to be labeled ice cream, or at least 8% if it contains extras, such as chocolate bits. Many premium scoops are even higher in fat.

Flavors range from elegant chocolate mousse and dulce de leche to Chunky Monkey (nutty, fudgy banana), with new ones being created constantly.

ICE MILK Similar to ice cream except that it contains less milk fat and milk solids. It is often considered the dieter's choice.

ICES Known as GRANITE in France and GRANITA in Italy, ices are a simple frozen mixture of sugar, water, and flavoring such as fruit juice, coffee, or wine. The ratio is usually 4 parts liquid to 1 part sugar. Rather than being scooped, the ices are shaved into shards with the tip of a spoon and mounded into a glass or goblet.

MARQUIS A chilled mousse-and-cake layered dessert. The most famous version is known as marquise au chocolat.

NEAPOLITAN A loaf of ice cream, typically with three layers: chocolate, vanilla, and strawberry.

SHERBET A very smooth frozen ice made from fruit, sugar, and either milk or egg whites.

SORBET In Italy, it is called sorbetto. A smooth frozen ice made with fruit purees (no dairy). Slightly sweetened and even savory ones are often served between courses to refresh the palate.

CROWN IT WITH CREAM

There's nothing quite like a scoop of rich homemade whipped cream to top off a dessert or even a freshly brewed cup of coffee. And fortunately the range of choices is vast:

HEAVY WHIPPING CREAM The crème de crème of them all! Containing 36% to 40% milk fat, it whips up fast and stiff. Occasionally pastry chefs stabilize it with a little (melted) gelatin before piping onto pies and cakes. Also sold under the name of heavy cream. Expect whipping cream to double in volume when whipped (a half pint or 1 cup heavy cream = 2 cups whipped cream).

LIGHT WHIPPING CREAM This readily available cream has a milk fat content of 30% to 36% and sometimes contains stabilizers and emulsifiers.

LIGHT CREAM (also COFFEE or TABLE CREAM) is the lightest cream of all, weighing in at 18% to 30% milk fat but more commonly 20%.

CLOTTED CREAM This specialty comes from Devonshire, England, and it is also known as Devon cream. It's made by heating very rich unpasteurized milk until a semisolid layer of cream forms on the surface. Once cooled, the thickened cream is scooped off and served with scones, jam, and a pot of steaming tea for a typical English "cream tea." It's also a popular topping for fresh fruits.

CRÈME FRAÎCHE This specialty comes from France, where it is made from unpasteurized cream that contains the bacteria needed to thicken it naturally. In America, where all cream must be pasteurized, crème fraîche is made by combining 2 tablespoons of sour cream or buttermilk to each cup of whipping cream. Crème fraîche is perfect over fresh fruit, warm cobblers, and puddings. Since crème fraîche doesn't curdle when boiled, it's ideal for lacing hot sauces or soups.

WHIPPED CREAM TO GO

There are two different types that are real time savers.

PRESSURIZED WHIPPED CREAM Look for this in aerosol cans in original, extra creamy, light, and even rich chocolate flavors. Yes, it's real whipped cream, usually with sugar, emulsifiers, stabilizers, and gas (such as nitrous oxide). It's not really whipped, but resembles whipped cream for it's released from the can in airy swirls. When buying, read the label and look for the word "cream." Some aerosol dessert toppings (often made with hydrogenated vegetable oils) contain no cream at all.

FROZEN WHIPPED TOPPING IN A TUB These tubs of whipped topping are popular as a fast, spoonable topping for desserts, as well as a versatile ingredient in many refrigerated no-bake desserts. Strawberry flavor is available in the spring and summer and French vanilla during the fall and winter.

COLOR IT CHOCOLATE

The real news in the chocolate aisles today is the availability of top-quality chocolate. It can lend a terrific, rich flavor to many no-bake creations.

IMPORTED BAKING CHOCOLATE You can find imported baking chocolate in gourmet stores. It contains pure cocoa butter and natural vanilla. It's a little more expensive but superb for cooking, with fine melting properties. Look for these varieties: unsweetened (100% pure cacao pâté), bittersweet (61–72% cocoa butter), gianduja (29% cocoa butter and 32% hazelnut), noir

Cooking Basics

CAKE 'N' CREAM

Cake in a no-bake book? Absolutely. There are excellent ways to have your cake, without baking it. We've scouted the marketplace and found that buttery-tasting pound cakes, both plain and chocolate swirl, can be found at your local bakery or in your grocer's bakery section or frozen food case. Always keep one on hand in your freezer, as it's all that's needed for Dessert in a Dash any day of the week. Here are some ways to transform a slice of cake into dessert (each makes four servings):

OODLES OF BERRIES Spread one side of 4 slices of pound cake with a thin coating of whipped cream cheese and place on dessert plates. Toss 1 cup of sliced strawberries, ½ cup of raspberries, and ½ cup of blueberries with 2 to 3 tablespoons of superfine sugar (depending upon how sweet the berries are) and some slivers of fresh mint leaves. Let the berries stand about 10 min-

utes, just until they begin to release their juices. Then spoon over the cake slices, scooping up the juices too. Garnish each with toasted sliced almonds and a mint sprig.

STRAWBERRY PATCH Spread one side of 4 slices of pound cake with a thin coating of raspberry jam. Hull and slice a pint of fresh strawberries into a bowl, sprinkle with 2 to 3 tablespoons of superfine sugar, and drizzle with a little crème de cassis (red currant liqueur). Let stand 10 minutes. Plate each cake slice and top with 2 scoops of raspberry sorbet and a generous helping of berries. Finish off each one with puffs of whipped cream, and sprinkle with a little cinnamon.

TRIPLE SPLIT Cut three ripe bananas into 4 pieces, then cut each piece horizontally in half, giving you 12 pieces. Place in a microwave-safe dish, sprinkle with some brown sugar, and microwave on High for a few seconds until the

sugar melts and the bananas are warm. On plates, top 4 slices of pound cake with 3 banana pieces each, then a scoop of chocolate ice cream and another of butter pecan. Drizzle with butterscotch ice cream sauce and sprinkle with coconut.

BLACK OUT! Put 4 slices of chocolate swirl pound cake on dessert plates and top with a double scoop of double Dutch fudge ice cream. Sprinkle with a few miniature chocolate chips and drizzle with hot fudge sauce. Top with dollops of whipped cream and chocolate sprinkles.

CAPPUCCINO CRAZE Sprinkle one side of each of 4 slices of pound cake with a little brewed coffee and set each on a plate. Top with 2 scoops of coffee ice cream and drizzle with chocolate sauce. Finish them off with a generous spoonful of whipped cream and a sprinkling of cinnamon. Garnish each with a thin chocolate mint.

orange, and ivoire (white) chocolate. You can often use bittersweet, semisweet, and sweet chocolate interchangeably in recipes—but not milk chocolate, due to the milk protein it contains.

DOMESTIC BAKING CHOCOLATE At your grocery store, fine chocolate is easy to find: unsweetened (50% to 58% of cocoa butter) and bittersweet, semisweet, or sweet chocolate, with increasing amounts of sugar added, as well

ICE CREAM SANDWICHES—YOUR WAY

In the 1890s on the streets of New York City, ice cream sandwiches began showing up on what was probably some of the first food vendor carts. The sandwiches consisted of two cakelike cookies with a slab of ice cream sandwiched in between. And on the opposite coast in San Francisco, similar sandwiches were also being enjoyed, but these were made with oatmeal cookies instead. Later in the twentieth century, the Chipwich was marketed: a sandwich that was similar to earlier versions but made with chocolate chip cookies.

Today the ice cream sandwich is experiencing a revival of sorts. Chefs are having a heyday, creating their own delicious cookies, from chocolate to butter cookies and everything in between. And, of course, the ice cream center changes with the seasons. The sandwiches are rolled in everything from graham-cracker crumbs to chopped peanuts and colorful sprinkles.

When making your own cre-ations, a good way to guard against the cookies crumbling is to choose ones that are big enough to hold the ice cream without it seeping out the sides, at least 3½ inches in diameter. Be sure they're thick and firm, not soft or delicate. For the fastest sandwich making ever, pack the ice cream into 12-ounce juice containers. Unmold it, then slice the ice cream with a warm knife and place it between the cookies.

Here are some fun sandwich combinations for you to try; then start creating your own.

PEANUT GOBBLERS To make each sandwich, take 2 large crisp peanut butter cookies (flat sides in) and sandwich about ½ cup chocolate ice cream in between. Roll the sides in finely chopped peanuts. Wrap each one in plastic wrap and store in the freezer.

LOTS OF DOTS For each sandwich, take 2 large crisp chocolate cookies (flat sides in) and sandwich about ½ cup cookie dough ice cream in between. Roll the sides in miniature candy-coated chocolate baking bits (all colors!). Wrap individually in plastic wrap and store in the freezer.

SICILIAN BREAKFAST BAGUETTE For each sandwich, split 1 brioche horizontally. Spoon about ⅓ cup coffee or lemon gelato on the bottom half and cover with the top. Eat immediately or wrap in plastic wrap and store in the freezer.

ICE CREAM SANDWICH PARISIENNE Start with a croissant for each sandwich. Split it horizontally and fill with about ¾ cup French vanilla ice cream. Drizzle with about 1 tablespoon hot fudge sauce, cover with the top, then wrap in plastic wrap and freeze.

GEORGIA PEACH For each sandwich, spread the bottoms of 2 large sugar cookies with raspberry preserves. Put about ½ cup peach ice cream on the jam side of 1 cookie, top with the other, jam side in. Wrap in plastic wrap and store in the freezer.

as unsweetened liquid chocolate. The liquid type is easier to use. But since it's made with vegetable oil rather than cocoa butter, it has less chocolate flavor.

WHITE CHOCOLATE Not really chocolate at all, it lacks chocolate liquor and thus has little chocolate flavor. It's actually a mixture of sugar, cocoa butter, milk solids, lecithin, and vanilla.

COOL CREATIONS

For keeping little hands busy in the summertime, pick up one of those nostalgic snow cone machines so your kids can make some fruity, cool, icy treats on those hot summer days. They'll think they're at the circus or state fair as they hand-crank these crushed icy favorites. You can easily buy the traditional snow cone syrups, too, so there's no cooking needed (just a lot of cranking!). Also look for frozen pop kits, complete with molds and built-in sticks for kids to make their own popsicles (great with watermelon). The molds come with a stand that keeps them upright in the freezer, ready to grab at a moment's notice. Plus there are even handy ice cream sandwich makers that make cutting out the cookies and molding the ice cream in-between a breeze.

Kaleidoscope Pops, page 48

S'MORES MAKER

Recreate those days around the campfire by picking up one of the S'mores makers on the market. It comes with its own marshmallow toasting grill, ceramic holders for all the S'mores fixin's (graham crackers, chocolate, and marshmallows), individual toasting forks, and a ceramic tray that holds it altogether. With this little kit, you can enjoy this favorite classic indoors or out. The best part: it's reasonably priced. Great for the little ones who are camp age, and for you too!

Browse through the *No-Bake Desserts* recipes and plan which one to try for dinner tonight. Here are some of our favorites:

Chocolate S'mores Fondue, page 130

Cherry Chocolate Shortcakes (page 29)

Fruity Parfaits (page 50)

Peanut Butter S'mores (page 72)

Cool 'n' Creamy Chocolate Pie (page 80)

Blushing Snowballs (page 105)

Cherry Cheese Heart (page 116)

Bake Not Brownie Bars (page 129)

Strawberry Chiffon Pie, page 76

Dessert Waffles, page 30

Fix 'em Fast!

Here's dessert, quick as a wink—without much fuss at all. And yummy enough that folks will ask for seconds. Whether you crave a bowl of pudding, a chewy chocolate cookie, or a piece of heavenly fudge, you'll find it here. For something different, whip up some heavenly ambrosia or serve a waffle smothered with fresh fruit. They're all fast to prepare, fun to serve, and easy on the pocketbook. And naturally, the best part is: you don't have to turn on the oven. We've also included instant fruit sauces to heat up in your microwave and some fabulous fast toppings that turn a slice of pound cake into delicious shortcake. They'll make you glad you found a few minutes to fix dessert!

SuperQuick
WARM MAPLE NUT SUNDAES

Prep **10 MINUTES**   *Cook* **15 MINUTES**

1   cup maple-flavored pancake syrup

2   tablespoons lemon juice

1   tablespoon butter or margarine

¼   teaspoon salt

4   1-inch slices banana bread

1   pint vanilla ice cream

Canned whipped dessert topping

¼   cup chopped walnuts

4   maraschino cherries (optional)

Use leftover banana bread or a loaf you've bought at the bakery to make this unusual sundae. You can use other ice cream flavors and different nuts, too. Try butter pecan ice cream and garnish with chopped pecans or toffee ice cream garnished with sliced almonds.

LET'S BEGIN Combine the first 4 ingredients in a medium saucepan and cook over medium heat for 15 minutes or until thickened, stirring frequently.

DRIZZLE & SERVE Place the banana bread on serving plates and top each one with a scoop of the ice cream. Drizzle evenly with the maple sauce and top with the whipped cream, walnuts, and a cherry, if you wish.

Makes 4 servings

Per serving: 694 calories, 8g protein, 111g carbohydrates, 26g fat, 9g saturated fat, 95mg cholesterol, 537mg sodium

Time Savers

SUNDAES IN A FLASH

The first ice cream sundae was created sometime in the 1800s. Back then, the favorite soda fountain treat was an ice cream soda, but blue laws prohibited the sale of carbonated drinks on Sunday. So clever soda fountain owners topped ice cream with syrup to create a "dry" sundae and changed the spelling so as not to offend the local church.

Create your own sundae keeping a few proportions in mind: a sundae is best with two generous scoops of ice cream to 3 to 4 tablespoons of syrup or fruit sauce, plus your own pick of extras.

ICE CREAM, FROZEN YO-GURT, OR GELATO—vanilla, chocolate, coffee, lemon, hazelnut, strawberry, peach, maple-walnut, pistachio, or cherry vanilla

NUTS FOR SPRINKLING—sliced almonds, toasted walnuts or hazelnuts, pumpkin seeds, or cashews

SYRUPS AND SAUCES—hot fudge sauce, maple syrup, fruit-flavored pancake syrups, or caramel sauce

EXTRAS—fresh berries, sliced peaches or chunks of ripe pineapple, crumbled oatmeal or chocolate sandwich cookies, crushed peppermint candy, toasted coconut, crushed peanut brittle, or M&M's

THE CROWNING TOUCH—whipped cream—plain, slightly sweetened, or flavored with vanilla, cinnamon, espresso powder, maple sugar, or bourbon

SuperQuick
ANGEL FOOD AMBROSIA

Prep **5 MINUTES**

1   can (15¼ ounces) fruit cocktail in heavy syrup

1   tablespoon frozen orange juice concentrate, thawed

1   cup frozen whipped dessert topping, thawed

4   slices angel food cake

¼   cup toasted coconut

In Greek mythology, ambrosia was the food of the gods on Mount Olympus. Today, ambrosia is usually a mix of bananas and orange segments tossed with lots of shredded coconut. Here, easy canned fruit cocktail, OJ concentrate, whipped topping, store-bought angel food cake, and coconut become food for the gods once again.

LET'S BEGIN Drain the fruit, reserving 2 tablespoons syrup. Stir the reserved syrup and orange juice concentrate into the dessert topping in a small bowl.

TOP & SERVE Spoon drained fruit over the cake. Top with the orange mixture. Sprinkle with coconut.

>*Makes 4 servings*
>
>*Per serving: 329 calories, 3g protein, 47g carbohydrates, 15g fat, 13g saturated fat, 0mg cholesterol, 253mg sodium*

FAST CHOCOLATE-ALMOND FUDGE

Prep **20 MINUTES**   *Cook* **10 MINUTES + CHILLING**

2½   cups sugar

½   cup butter or margarine

1   can (5 ounces) evaporated milk

1   package (12 ounces) semisweet chocolate morsels

¾   cup toasted, slivered almonds

1   teaspoon vanilla extract

Drenched with butter and chocolate, and gilded with toasted almonds, this fudge is a blue ribbon winner.

LET'S BEGIN Line a 9-inch square pan with buttered foil. Combine the sugar, butter, and evaporated milk in a large saucepan. Bring to a boil, stirring constantly. Continue to boil over medium heat for 5 minutes, stirring constantly.

STIR & CHILL Remove from the heat and stir in the chocolate. Blend until smooth. Stir in the almonds and vanilla. Pour into the prepared pan and refrigerate, covered, for at least 2 hours. Remove fudge from pan by pulling out and removing the foil. Cut into squares and serve.

>*Makes 25 squares*
>
>*Per square: 50 calories, 1g protein, 6g carbohydrates, 3g fat, 1g saturated fat, 4mg cholesterol, 2mg sodium*

DOUBLE-DIP STRAWBERRIES

Prep **15 MINUTES**   *Microwave* **1 MINUTE + CHILLING**

1   package (10 ounces)
    white chocolate chips

2   tablespoons shortening
    (do not substitute
    butter, margarine,
    spread, or oil)

1   cup semisweet chocolate
    chips

4   cups fresh strawberries,
    rinsed, patted dry, and
    chilled

Any occasion becomes a fancy affair when you serve these breath-taking berries. If your guests only knew how easy they are to make!

LET'S BEGIN Line a tray with waxed paper. Place the white chocolate chips and 1 tablespoon of shortening in a medium microwave-safe bowl. Microwave on High for 1 minute and stir until the chips are melted and the mixture is smooth. If necessary, microwave for an additional 30 seconds at a time, just until smooth when stirred.

DIP & CHILL Holding each strawberry by the top, dip ⅔ of each one into the white chocolate mixture. Shake gently to remove the excess chocolate. Place on the prepared tray and refrigerate for 30 minutes or until the chocolate is firm. Repeat the melting procedure with semisweet chocolate chips and the remaining 1 tablespoon shortening in a clean microwave-safe bowl. Dip the lower ⅓ of each berry into the semisweet chocolate mixture. Refrigerate for 30 minutes or until the chocolate is firm. Cover and refrigerate any leftover strawberries.

Makes 2 dozen strawberries

Per strawberry: 120 calories, 1g protein, 13g carbohydrates, 7g fat, 4g saturated fat, 2mg cholesterol, 14mg sodium

NO-BAKE FUDGE COOKIES

Prep **15 MINUTES**   *Microwave* **5 MINUTES + CHILLING**

½   **cup butter or margarine, cut into pieces**

½   **cup milk**

2   **cups sugar**

⅓   **cup unsweetened cocoa**

1   **teaspoon salt**

1   **teaspoon vanilla extract**

4   **cups quick-cooking oats**

Quick-cooking oats add a hearty and satisfying chewiness to these super-easy microwave cookies. We love them hot and fragrant with glasses of ice-cold milk on the side.

LET'S BEGIN Line a tray or cookie sheet with waxed paper. Combine the butter and milk in a large microwaveable bowl. Microwave on High (100%) for 1 minute or until butter melts when stirred. Stir in the sugar and cocoa until well blended. Microwave on High for 1½ minutes, then stir. Microwave on High an additional 1½ to 3 minutes or until sugar is completely dissolved and mixture is hot and bubbly on the surface. Carefully stir in the salt, vanilla, and oats.

OFF THE SPOON Drop the mixture by tablespoons onto the prepared tray. Flatten each slightly with the back of the spoon. Let cookies stand until firm. If necessary, cover and refrigerate until firm.

Makes 3 dozen cookies

Per cookie: 104 calories, 1g protein, 17g carbohydrates, 3g fat, 2g saturated fat, 8mg cholesterol, 85mg sodium

Cook to Cook

HOW CAN I MAKE ICE CREAM SODAS AT HOME?

" I love to make bubbly, frothy ice cream sodas at home. They are always such a special treat.

To make one, take a small scoop of ice cream and stir it with about 3 tablespoons flavored syrup in the bottom of a tall glass. Add chilled seltzer, top with a large scoop of ice cream, and add whipped cream.

For a Broadway Soda, use 3 tablespoons chocolate syrup, 2 scoops of coffee ice cream, and chilled seltzer up to the top of the glass.

For a Black & White, use 3 tablespoons chocolate syrup, 2 scoops of vanilla ice cream, and chilled seltzer up to the top of the glass.

For a Brown Cow, use 2 tablespoons chocolate syrup, 2 scoops of vanilla ice cream, and chilled, frothy root beer to the top of the glass.

For a Creamsicle Soda, use 3 tablespoons vanilla syrup, 2 scoops of vanilla ice cream, and chilled orange soda to the top of the glass. "

SuperQuick
WHITE CHOCOLATE CLUSTERS

Prep **5 MINUTES**   *Cook* **1 MINUTE + CHILLING**

1   package (12 ounces) white chocolate morsels

1   package (6 ounces) sweetened dried cranberries

½   cup chopped walnuts or pecans, optional

⅓   cup shredded coconut, optional

LET'S BEGIN Line a cookie sheet with foil and set aside. Place the chocolate in a microwaveable bowl. Microwave at Medium-High (70%) for 1 minute, stirring after 30 seconds. Microwave for an additional 10 to 20 seconds or until the chocolate is completely melted. Stir in the remaining ingredients until thoroughly combined.

OFF THE SPOON Drop the chocolate mixture by rounded teaspoonfuls on to the prepared cookie sheet. Chill for 20 minutes, or until the clusters harden. Store in a tightly sealed container in the refrigerator. The clusters may be stored in the refrigerator up to 2 weeks.

Makes about 16 clusters

Per cluster: 141 calories, 1g protein, 22g carbohydrates, 6g fat, 5g saturated fat, 0mg cholesterol, 30mg sodium

SuperQuick

SUPER POWER CRUNCH BARS

Prep **5 MINUTES**   *Microwave* **2 MINUTES + COOLING**

⅓   cup honey

2   tablespoons butter or
      margarine

4   cups marshmallows

6   cups honey-coated oat
      puffed cereal

1   cup dried apricots,
      chopped

1   cup almonds, chopped

We like to individually wrap these super-fabulous energy bars so they are ready to drop into a lunchbox, brown bag lunch, backpack, or purse. They're high in flavor and low in calories—the perfect combination.

LET'S BEGIN Mix the honey and butter in a large microwaveable bowl and microwave on High for 1 minute. Stir the mixture well. Add the marshmallows and toss to coat. Microwave for 1½ minutes or until the marshmallows are puffed. Add the remaining ingredients and mix well.

PRESS & CUT Pour the cereal mixture into a greased 13 × 9-inch baking pan; press firmly. Cool for 15 minutes. Cut into 24 bars.

Makes 24 bars

Per bar: 130 calories, 2g protein, 24g carbohydrates, 4g fat, 1g saturated fat, 5mg cholesterol, 85mg sodium

24   **NO-BAKE DESSERTS**

SuperQuick
BANANA KIWI PUDDING
Prep **10 MINUTES**   Cook **8 MINUTES**

You can use almost any variety of leftover cooked rice for this heart-warming pudding: brown, basmati, jasmine, and regular long-grain will all be great. Be sure to use pure vanilla extract—not imitation—for the most delicious flavor.

1⅓   cups cooked rice

1⅓   cups skim milk

Low-calorie sugar substitute to equal 2 tablespoons
     sugar

1   teaspoon vanilla extract

1   large ripe banana

½   cup frozen, fat-free whipped topping

Thawed kiwifruit, sliced, for garnish

LET'S BEGIN Combine the rice and milk in a medium saucepan and cook, stirring frequently over medium heat, for 5 to 8 minutes or until the mixture is smooth and creamy. Remove from the heat and cool. Stir in the sugar substitute and vanilla.

FINAL TOUCH Just before serving, mash the banana. Fold the banana and whipped topping into the pudding. Garnish with kiwifruit slices.

> *Makes 4 servings*
> *Per serving: 155 calories, 5g protein, 29g carbohydrates, 2g fat, 2g saturated fat, 2mg cholesterol, 237mg sodium*

On the Menu

Travel from region to region in America and you'll be delighted with the fast sweets that are in store, all along the way.

NORTHEAST
Main Blueberry Pudding

Caramelized Apple Wedges with Vanilla Ice Cream

SOUTH
Snow on the Mountain

Lemon Syllabub

Bananas Flambé

Fresh Strawberry Shortcakes with Cream Biscuits

MIDWEST
Wild Grape Dumplings

Quilting Bee Apple Turnovers

WEST
Fruit Ice

Peach Surprise

EASY PEANUT BUTTER CHOCOLATE CHEESECAKE PIE

Prep **20 MINUTES**   *Microwave* **2 MINUTES**   *Chill* **1 HOUR**

1   package (6 ounces) prepared chocolate crumb crust

¼   cup + 2 tablespoons unsalted peanuts, chopped

2   tablespoons caramel topping

1   package (11 ounces) peanut butter & milk chocolate morsels

¼   cup milk

1   package (8 ounces) cream cheese, softened

¼   cup confectioners' sugar

1½ cups frozen whipped topping, thawed

Three favorite things, whipped up into one great pie: chocolate, peanut butter, and peanuts.

LET'S BEGIN Sprinkle ¼ cup of the peanuts onto the crust bottom. Drizzle with 1 tablespoon of caramel topping.

MICROWAVE & MIX Microwave the morsels and milk in a medium microwave-safe bowl on Medium-High (70%) power for 45 seconds. Stir until smooth, microwaving an additional 10 seconds at a time, if necessary.

CHILL & SERVE Beat the cream cheese and sugar in a large bowl with an electric mixer on high until smooth. Beat in the chocolate mixture. Fold in the whipped topping and spoon into the pie crust. Sprinkle with the remaining peanuts, and drizzle with the remaining caramel topping. Cover and chill for at least 1 hour.

Makes 8 servings

Per serving: 511 calories, 7g protein, 49g carbohydrates, 34g fat, 17g saturated fat, 39mg cholesterol, 248mg sodium

---

Food Facts

CHEESECAKES ARE **NOT** ALL CREATED EQUAL

Over the years, two basic kinds of cheesecakes have evolved. The Italian type closely resembles cakes that have been made for centuries in Europe. They are usually made from ricotta cheese and prepared in a pastry crust, often with bits of candied fruits scattered throughout. The texture is dry and airy and the cakes typically bake up quite a bit higher than the other type.

In the early twentieth century, a phenomenon occurred in the Jewish neighborhoods of New York City. A smooth, silky rich, creamy cheesecake appeared at Arnold Reuben's Restaurant on 58th Street. Soon, other Jewish restaurants began serving similar cakes, all smooth, dense, incredibly creamy, and rich—but each with a distinctive difference from their competitors'. Junior's Restaurant in

Brooklyn serves a creamy cheesecake with a thin cake-like crust, while Lindy's, introduced in 1940, popularized a thick cookie crust. Some are served with a thin coating of sour cream on top, while others have fruit toppings, or nothing at all.

And while many classic recipes include eggs and call for baking, a lot of no-bake cheesecakes are equally delicious.

EASY TIRAMISU

Prep **20 MINUTES + CHILLING**

1   package (2.8 ounces) mocha mousse mix

⅔   cup milk

1   cup espresso or strong coffee, at room temperature

1   tablespoon brandy, or 2 teaspoons brandy extract

2   packages (3 to 3.5 ounces) ladyfingers

Shaved or grated chocolate

In Italian, tiramisu means "pick me up." And no dessert lifts one's spirits as well as this creamy mocha and ladyfinger dream concoction. Mocha mousse mix shaves lots of time off the prep.

LET'S BEGIN Prepare the mousse mix according to the package directions using ⅔ cup milk. Combine the coffee and brandy in a pie plate. Dip the ladyfingers into the mixture.

LAYER IT Line the bottom of a 9-inch square dish with half the moistened ladyfingers. Spoon half the mousse over the ladyfingers and top with the remaining ladyfingers. Spoon the remaining mousse over the top. Sprinkle with chocolate. Refrigerate for 2 hours before serving.

Makes 9 servings

Per serving: 135 calories, 3g protein, 18g carbohydrates, 5g fat, 3g saturated fat, 71mg cholesterol, 66mg sodium

---

Cooking Basics

5 WAYS TO TOP SHORTCAKES

Don't be fooled into thinking that shortcakes are just a warm-weather treat. They can be enjoyed winter, spring, summer, and fall. Either bake a triple batch of your favorite shortcakes and freeze until ready to use, or purchase prepared shortcakes in the bakery section of your supermarket.

GINGER-PEAR SHORTCAKES Sauté peeled and sliced ripe pears in butter and sugar until tender and golden. Add a small amount of finely chopped crystallized ginger. Use to fill the shortcakes and top with nutmeg-scented whipped cream.

GRILLED PEACH SHORT-CAKES are a nice change of pace. Brush the tops of shortcakes with melted butter and sprinkle with cinnamon sugar. Cut ripe peaches into wedges, brush with butter, and grill until tender. Toss with fresh lemon juice and sugar. Use to fill the shortcakes and top with vanilla whipped cream.

RHUBARB AND RASP-BERRY SHORTCAKES Dice the rhubarb and cook with cornstarch and sugar just until tender—it should still hold its shape. Gently combine with some fresh raspberries and use to fill shortcakes. Crown with cinnamon whipped cream.

CHOCOLATE-CHERRY SHORTCAKES Split the shortcakes and fill with lightly drained cherry pie filling. Sprinkle with miniature chocolate chips and cover. Top with sweetened whipped cream and chocolate curls or shavings.

APPLE-CARAMEL SHORT-CAKES Split and fill shortcakes with apple pie filling. Drizzle jarred caramel sauce over the dessert plates, top each with a shortcake, and dollop whipped cream over all.

CHERRY CHOCOLATE SHORTCAKE

Prep **20 MINUTES + CHILLING**

1   **frozen pound cake loaf (10¾ ounces), thawed**

1   **can (21 ounces) cherry pie filling, chilled**

1   **container (8 ounces) frozen whipped topping, thawed**

⅓   **cup unsweetened cocoa**

½   **cup confectioners' sugar**

The convenience of frozen pound cake, prepared pie filling, and ready-made whipped topping make this one of the easiest—and most impressive—desserts you'll ever make.

LET'S BEGIN Slice the pound cake horizontally into three layers. Place the bottom layer on a serving plate and top with half of the pie filling, using mostly the cherries from the filling. Repeat with the middle cake layer and the remaining cherries from the pie filling. Top with the rounded cake layer. Cover and refrigerate for 2 hours.

FROST & SERVE Place the whipped topping in a medium bowl. Sift the cocoa and the confectioners' sugar into the bowl with the whipped topping. Stir until smooth and well blended. Immediately spread the mixture over the top and sides of cake, covering it completely. Refrigerate until ready to serve. Store any leftover cake in the refrigerator.

Makes 6 servings

Per serving: 466 calories, 4g protein, 74g carbohydrates, 17g fat, 13g saturated fat, 112mg cholesterol, 221mg sodium

DESSERT WAFFLES

Prep **20 MINUTES**   *Cook* **2 MINUTES**

1   package (10 ounces) frozen red raspberries in light syrup, thawed

12   small frozen Belgian waffles

3   cups assorted fresh fruit (such as blackberries, blueberries, sliced kiwifruit, and strawberries)

1½   cups frozen whipped topping, thawed

Topped with fresh fruit and a ruby red raspberry sauce, waffles make a lovely, yet easy, summer dessert. Make a double batch of the sauce and use it for topping all kinds of sweets—pound cake, cheesecake, or ice cream.

LET'S BEGIN Place the raspberries in a blender or food processor and process until smooth. Press the mixture through a fine wire mesh strainer if you wish, to remove the seeds.

HEAT & SERVE Prepare the waffles according to package directions. Serve the waffles topped with the raspberry sauce, fruit, and whipped topping.

Makes 12 servings

Per serving: 176 calories, 3g protein, 30g carbohydrates, 5g fat, 3g saturated fat, 0mg cholesterol, 272mg sodium

Cooking Basics

BLENDER FRUIT SAUCES

With a blender, some fruit (fresh or canned), lime or lemon juice, and sugar, fabulous fruit sauces are well on their way to topping sundaes, brightening up angel food cake, moistening a fruit salad, or flavoring a sweet fruit smoothie.

Tips: We like to sweeten with superfine sugar, as it dissolves instantly. If you have any left-over sauce, store it covered in the refrigerator and use it within a week.

Here are some of our favorites:

BLUEBERRY-CASSIS SAUCE Put 1 pint fresh blueberries into a blender with ¼ cup crème de cassis (red currant liqueur). Whirl until pureed. Sweeten to taste and finish with a splash of fresh lemon juice. Makes about 1½ cups.

RASPBERRY SAUCE Put 3 cups fresh raspberries into a blender and puree until smooth. Press the sauce through a sieve set over a bowl; discard the seeds. Add fresh lemon juice and sugar to taste. Makes about 2 cups.

STRAWBERRY-LIME SAUCE Put 1 pint fresh strawberries, hulled and halved, into a blender with ¼ cup light corn syrup. Puree until smooth. Add fresh lime juice to taste and additional corn syrup, if needed. Makes about 1½ cups.

RED PLUM SAUCE Put 6 pitted and chopped large ripe red plums (about 1½ pounds) into a blender. Puree until smooth. Add sugar and fresh lemon juice to taste. Makes about 1½ cups.

SuperQuick
QUICK PUMPKIN PUDDING
Prep **10 MINUTES + COOLING**

1   package (5$\frac{1}{10}$ ounces)
     vanilla instant pudding
     and pie filling mix

1   can (12 ounces)
     evaporated milk

1   can (15 ounces) pure
     pumpkin (not pumpkin
     pie mix)

1   teaspoon pumpkin pie
     spice

1   pint whipping cream,
     whipped to soft peaks

When you're longing for pumpkin pie but haven't the time or inclination, serve up this spicy dessert from your pantry. All you need is the whipped cream, but frozen whipped topping is a cool substitute.

LET'S BEGIN Beat the pudding mix and evaporated milk in a large bowl, according to package directions. Refrigerate for 5 minutes. Mix in the pumpkin and pumpkin pie spice. Spoon the pudding into dessert dishes. Refrigerate for 10 minutes or until ready to serve. Top with whipped cream.

Makes 8 servings

Per serving: 344 calories, 3g protein, 23g carbohydrates, 25g fat, 16g saturated fat, 86mg cholesterol, 290mg sodium

CHOCOLATE TRUFFLES

Prep **10 MINUTES**   *Cook* **4 MINUTES + CHILLING**

1½ cups semisweet chocolate morsels

½ cup jellied cranberry sauce

2 tablespoons whipping cream

2 tablespoons unsweetened cocoa

1½ tablespoons confectioners' sugar

It just wouldn't be the holidays without chocolate truffles. Jellied cranberry sauce makes these truffles special. We like to place them in silver or gold candy cups so the truffles are at their festive best.

LET'S BEGIN Place the chocolate, cranberry sauce, and cream in a medium saucepan. Stir over medium-low heat for 3 to 4 minutes until the sauce is smooth, whisking frequently. Remove from the heat and pour into a glass or plastic bowl. Cover with plastic wrap. Let stand at room temperature to thicken.

SHAPE & CHILL Sprinkle the cocoa onto a small plate. Scoop out a rounded teaspoonful of the chocolate mixture. Roll in the cocoa, coating thoroughly. Dust your hands with the confectioners' sugar. Roll truffles in your hands to form 1-inch balls. Arrange truffles on a serving plate. Chill 30 minutes.

Makes 30 truffles

Per truffle: 56 calories, 1g protein, 7g carbohydrates, 3g fat, 2g saturated fat, 1mg cholesterol, 1mg sodium

Luscious Lemony Fruit "Shortcakes," page 40

Fresh Fruit Endings

Nothing's quite as easy and delicious as ending a meal with fresh fruit. These desserts are practically guaranteed to be light, sweet, and bursting with fabulous flavor. Our collection has it all: shortcakes and creamy tarts, rich yogurt parfaits, and even fun pops—all made delicious with ripe, fragrant fruits. For a special dinner, whip up a Raspberry Trifle ahead of time, layer a fresh berry trifle as they do in England, or stir up Bananas Foster while your guests watch (like they do in New Orleans). Another day, turn taco shells into fresh fruit desserts. You'll also find some fruit and cheese match-ups you can pick up on your way home. Think fresh fruit for dessert tonight!

CALIFORNIA FRUIT DIPS

Prep **15 MINUTES**

No need to remove the stems from these fresh berries—they make great "handles" for dipping. Since dips travel so well, keep this idea in mind for your next picnic or tailgate party.

3   pints fresh strawberries, washed and patted dry

STRAWBERRY CREAM DIP

½   cup reduced-fat sour cream

¼   cup strawberry (no sugar added) fruit spread or strawberry jam

CHOCOLATE FUDGE DIP

6   tablespoons nonfat yogurt

6   tablespoons prepared chocolate fudge sauce

1½   teaspoons frozen orange juice concentrate, thawed

HONEY ALMOND DIP

⅔   cup nonfat yogurt

3   tablespoons toasted, slivered almonds, finely chopped

2½   tablespoons honey

LET'S BEGIN For each dip, whisk ingredients in separate containers until smooth. Serve in small bowls to accompany strawberries.

Makes 6 servings

Per serving: 222 calories, 6g protein, 37g carbohydrates, 7g fat, 2g saturated fat, 9mg cholesterol, 108mg sodium

---

Cooking Basics

FRUIT 'N' CHEESE MATCH-UPS

When serving fruits and cheeses, consider the rest of the menu. A platter of fruit and cheeses at a light luncheon can be more substantial and indeed may become part of the main meal. On the other hand, fruit and cheeses as a dessert at the end of a rich, multi-course meal need to be simple, with only one or two selections to top off the evening. Naturally rich, creamy cheeses complement the stronger, harder varieties, and a crisp apple or fragrant grapes will round it all out. Here are a few fruit and cheese combos that we find work well together:

• Danish blue, mild Vermont Cheddar, an herb-coated chèvre (goat's cheese) with green seedless grapes and ripe pears.

• A classic French brie, a thick slice of fontina, and a wedge of Colby with dried figs, walnuts, and a crisp Granny Smith apple.

• A perfectly ripe Camembert, an English Cheddar, and a Swiss Gruyère with dark purple grapes and fresh ripe strawberries.

• A wedge of Jarlsberg, a brick of Danish Havarti, and some creamy Saint André with red seedless grapes, dried apricots, and a crisp Red Delicious apple.

SABAYON WITH FRESH FRUITS
Prep **10 MINUTES**   *Cook* **10 MINUTES + CHILLING**

1½   teaspoons unflavored gelatin

¼   cup cold water

⅔   cup fruity white wine such as Chardonnay

¼   cup sweet Marsala wine

½   cup sugar

3   large egg yolks

1   large egg

2   tablespoons lemon juice

1   tablespoon Grand Marnier liqueur

1   cup cold whipping cream, whipped

2   pints fresh berries, such as raspberries, blueberries, strawberries

Did you know that sabayon is the French word for zabaglione, which is considered by some to be one of Italy's great food gifts to the world? It is a light-as-a-feather dessert sauce that is made by beating egg yolks with sugar and a liqueur until thick and foamy. It is made even more spectacular by folding in whipped cream.

LET'S BEGIN Sprinkle the gelatin over cold water in a small cup and let stand until gelatin softens. Do not stir. Combine the softened gelatin, wines, sugar, egg yolks, egg, lemon juice, and liqueur in the top of a double boiler. Cook over gently simmering water, whisking constantly, 5 to 10 minutes or until mixture thickens and coats the back of a metal spoon.

CHILL & SERVE Place the top of the double boiler in a bowl of ice water and whisk mixture gently until cooled to room temperature. Fold in the whipped cream. Spoon the berries into 8 serving dishes and ladle the sabayon over the berries.

Makes 8 servings

Per serving: 237 calories, 3g protein, 21g carbohydrates, 14g fat, 8g saturated fat, 144mg cholesterol, 27mg sodium

GRILLED FRUIT KABOBS WITH TROPICAL YOGURT SAUCE

Prep **25 MINUTES**   *Cook* **10 MINUTES**

6   bamboo skewers, 8 to 10 inches long

1   container (6 ounces) key lime pie yogurt

1   package (3 ounces) cream cheese, softened

2   teaspoons sugar

⅛   teaspoon imitation coconut extract (optional)

1   tablespoon lime juice

1   tablespoon butter or margarine, melted

1   small pineapple, peeled and cored

1   pound large, fresh, firm strawberries

2   large, fresh, firm nectarines or peaches, pitted and cut into wedges

Kabobs are always fun and enjoyable, whether for an appetizer, main dish, or dessert, as we've done here. Be sure you use firm fruit, or it might not hold up to skewering and grilling.

LET'S BEGIN Preheat a gas or charcoal grill to medium heat. Soak the skewers in warm water for 10 minutes, then drain and set aside.

BLEND & CHILL Combine the yogurt, cream cheese, sugar, and coconut extract in an electric blender and blend until smooth. Cover and chill.

BRUSH & GRILL Mix the lime juice and melted butter in a small bowl. Set aside. Cut the pineapple into 1-inch thick slices, then quarter the slices. Remove the hulls (leaves) from the strawberries. Alternately thread the strawberries, pineapple, and nectarine wedges on skewers. Brush with the butter mixture. Grill the kabobs for 6 to 8 minutes or until heated through, turning once or twice. Do not allow strawberries to overcook. Remove the grilled fruit from the skewers and serve with yogurt dipping sauce.

Makes 6 servings

Per serving: 184 calories, 4g protein, 28g carbohydrates, 8g fat, 4g saturated fat, 22mg cholesterol, 74mg sodium

SuperQuick
CINNAMONY SPICED PEACHES

Prep **5 MINUTES**   *Cook* **10 MINUTES**

2   tablespoons light corn syrup

¼   teaspoon cinnamon

¼   teaspoon lemon juice

2   cans (16 ounces each) sliced peaches, drained, or 6 fresh peaches, peeled and sliced

These versatile and oh so delicious peaches are given just the right flavor with a touch of lemon and a pinch of cinnamon. You can use fresh peaches in season, but using the canned variety really cuts down on the kitchen time.

LET'S BEGIN Stir together the corn syrup, cinnamon, and lemon juice in a medium saucepan. Add the peaches and simmer, uncovered, 10 minutes.

FINAL TOUCH Spoon the peaches into serving dishes and serve hot or cold over ice cream, angel food cake, or pound cake.

> **Makes 4 servings**
>
> *Per serving: 92 calories, 1g protein, 24g carbohydrates, 0g fat, 0g saturated fat, 0mg cholesterol, 12mg sodium*

SuperQuick
BANANAS FOSTER

Prep **5 MINUTES**   *Cook* **10 MINUTES**

½   cup butter or margarine

½   cup firmly packed brown sugar

1   teaspoon imitation rum extract

½   teaspoon cinnamon

4   bananas, sliced into ¼-inch slices

Ice cream

Bananas Foster is a much-loved dessert that was created at Brennan's Restaurant in New Orleans in the 1950s. It was named for one of the restaurant's regular customers, Richard Foster. Thank you, Richard!

LET'S BEGIN Melt the butter in a large, heavy skillet. Add the sugar and stir until it dissolves. Stir in rum extract and cinnamon. Add the bananas to the skillet and cook for 2 minutes, stirring gently to coat banana slices.

FINAL TOUCH Place 1 or 2 scoops of ice cream in each serving dish and spoon the warm banana slices and sauce over the top. Serve immediately.

> **Makes 4 servings**
>
> *Per serving: 560 calories, 4g protein, 70g carbohydrates, 32g fat, 17g saturated fat, 94mg cholesterol, 238mg sodium*

Luscious Lemony Fruit "Shortcakes"

Prep **20 MINUTES + STANDING TIME**

⅓ cup plus 2 tablespoons prepared lemon curd

2 tablespoons water

4 cups cut-up fresh fruit

1 cup cold whipping cream

6 packaged sponge cake cups

No time to bake but still would love to serve shortcakes? Just pick up a package of those little sponge cake cups, line them with lemon curd, and fill them with fruits aplenty. Peaches, blueberries, raspberries, or sliced strawberries are perfect choices.

LET'S BEGIN Spoon 2 tablespoons of the lemon curd into a large bowl. Gradually stir in the water with a wire whisk until smooth. Add the fruit and toss gently to coat. Let stand for 15 to 20 minutes.

TOP & SERVE Beat the cream with the remaining ⅓ cup lemon curd in a small chilled bowl at high speed just until soft peaks form. To serve, place the sponge cake cups on individual dessert plates, then fill with the fruit mixture. Spoon the whipped cream over the top.

Makes 6 servings

Per serving: 390 calories, 5g protein, 48g carbohydrates, 21g fat, 12g saturated fat, 150mg cholesterol, 160mg sodium

---

Time Savers

CUTTING UP FRUIT AHEAD

There are lots of clever ways to prepare fruit ahead for a special fruit salad, a topping for a cake, or a filling for a pie or tart. Surprisingly, even pears and peaches can be prepared ahead! The key is to keep the fruit firm, juicy, and bright looking.

BERRIES Put berries into a colander and rinse under a light spray of cold water for about 30 seconds. Gently shake the colander to remove the excess water. Place the berries in a single layer on a double or triple thickness of paper towels in a shallow pan. Place a layer of paper towels over the berries (to absorb moisture) and cover with plastic wrap. Refrigerate up to several hours. **Tip**: Do not hull strawberries until ready to use, and place them stem down on the toweling.

TREE FRUIT (peaches, nectarines, apricots, apples, pears) should be rinsed and patted dry with paper towels. They can be diced or cut into wedges. Just toss them with some fresh lemon juice so they don't turn brown.

PINEAPPLE This hearty fruit can be peeled, chopped, diced, or sliced. Place in an airtight container up to a day ahead. Pat dry before using.

Apple Split

Prep **5 MINUTES**

1   **medium banana, peeled and split lengthwise**

2   **tablespoons low-fat whipped cream cheese**

¼   **cup fresh raspberries or any diced fresh fruit**

¼   **cup chunky style applesauce**

Chocolate syrup (optional)

What a treat for fruit lovers! This healthful dessert serves up a triple helping of fruit: a ripe banana and fresh raspberries topped with a generous measure of sweet-tart applesauce.

LET'S BEGIN Place the split banana in a shallow serving dish or on a plate. Dollop with the cream cheese and spoon the raspberries over the cheese. Top with the applesauce. Drizzle with the chocolate syrup, if desired.

Makes 1 serving

Per serving: 210 calories, 4g protein, 43g carbohydrates, 4g fat, 3g saturated fat, 10mg cholesterol, 60mg sodium

TINY FRUIT TARTS

Prep **15 MINUTES**   *Cook* **5 MINUTES**   *Chill* **1 HOUR**

1   package (3 ounces) vanilla pudding and pie filling mix (not instant)

⅓   cup water

1   can (12 ounces) evaporated low-fat milk

1   teaspoon grated lemon zest

6   prepared single-serving graham cracker crusts

2   cups cut-up fruit (such as kiwifruit, peaches, or pineapple), or berries (optional)

1   garnish of mint leaves (optional)

These are fun because each diner gets his or her own tart to enjoy. Be creative and arrange the fruit in a different design for each dessert, or use a single fruit for each tart and let guests choose the one they like the most.

LET'S BEGIN Combine the pudding mix and the water in a medium saucepan and stir until well mixed. Add the milk and lemon zest and stir until the mixture is smooth. Cook over medium-low heat for 5 minutes, stirring constantly, until the mixture comes to a boil and thickens.

CHILL & SERVE Spoon the filling evenly into the crusts and refrigerate for 1 hour or until set. Top with the fruit and garnish with mint leaves before serving, if you wish.

Makes 6 servings

Per serving: 227 calories, 2g protein, 29g carbohydrates, 7g fat, 2g saturated fat, 3mg cholesterol, 255mg sodium

KEY LIME TWIST

For a Key Lime twist to this recipe, substitute 2 teaspoons fresh lime juice and 1 teaspoon grated lime zest.

Cook to Cook

WHAT FRUITS SHOULD I USE FOR TOPPING TARTS?

"There are lots of great ways to use strawberries. If I can find small ones, I place them stem side down, otherwise I slice and place them in overlapping rows—very dramatic!

It's also nice to **paint the berries with melted strained** *apricot jam,* which makes them glisten like jewels. If peaches are looking good, I cut them into thin wedges and place them, cut side up. This is especially nice if the tart is round.

Another fun thing to do is **create a fruit "painting."**

I go to the best produce stand around and choose raspberries, currants, fresh mint, kiwifruit, gooseberries, star fruit, or other exotic items. I then decoratively arrange them in the tart just like a painting. Wow, is that ever spectacular!"

HONEY-ALMOND CREAM WITH BERRIES

Prep **15 MINUTES + CHILLING**

Fresh berries are always welcomed for dessert, but they're even more delicious when served with cream. These berries are topped with a creamy combo of cottage cheese and nonfat sour cream that's sweetened with honey. Dry-roasted almonds top it all, perfectly. It surprisingly weighs in at only 94 calories and 3 grams of fat per serving. If made completely with regular sour cream, it would be one-third more calories and more than double the fat.

1	cup 1% fat cottage cheese with no added salt
½	cup nonfat or light sour cream
¼	cup honey
½	teaspoon almond extract
2	cups fresh strawberries (1 pint)
1	cup fresh raspberries (½ pint)
1	cup fresh blueberries (½ pint)
½	cup slivered almonds, dry-roasted

LET'S BEGIN In a food processor or blender, process the cottage cheese for 1 minute. Scrape sides of container and process 1 minute longer or until smooth. Transfer to an airtight container and refrigerate for about 8 hours, or until firm.

CHILL & SERVE Spoon the cottage cheese into a medium mixing bowl and fold in the sour cream. Gently stir in the honey and almond extract (at this point the mixture is ready to serve or it can be refrigerated for up to two days in an airtight container). At serving time, remove the stems and leaves from the strawberries and slice into in a medium bowl. Carefully stir in the other berries. Spoon about ⅓ cup berries into 12 dessert dishes or goblets. Top each serving with 2 tablespoons of the cream mixture, then sprinkle with almonds.

Makes 12 servings

Per serving: 94 calories, 5g protein, 14g carbohydrates, 3g fat, 1g saturated fat, 3mg cholesterol, 21mg sodium

PINEAPPLE PECAN CUPS

Prep **10 MINUTES**   *Chill* **2 HOURS**

1   can (12 ounces)
     evaporated milk

1   cup chopped pecans

1   package (8 ounces)
     cream cheese, cut up

1   jar (12 ounces)
     pineapple preserves

Fresh pineapple wedges and
     mint leaves (optional)

A dessert that can best be described as super-fast and super-fabulous tasting. The blender does all the work and you get all the credit!

LET'S BEGIN Combine the first 4 ingredients in a blender and process until smooth. Spoon ½ cup of the mixture into each of 8 dessert cups or ramekins.

CHILL & SERVE Refrigerate for 2 hours or until chilled. Garnish with pineapple wedges and mint leaves, if you wish.

Makes 8 servings

Per serving: 367 calories, 4g protein, 33g carbohydrates, 23g fat, 9g saturated fat, 35mg cholesterol, 110mg sodium

---

Cooking Basics

CUTTING UP A FRESH PINEAPPLE

The first key step is to choose the right pineapple—one that's slightly soft and yellow-golden, not greenish. Most importantly, select fruit with a fragrant sweet aroma without any kind of fermented smell.

Leaves should be crisp, fresh, and green—not brown and dry. Contrary to what many believe, the ease with which you can pull out a leaf from the top doesn't indicate ripeness. It's all in the feel and the smell.

To cut perfectly clean, round slices of pineapple:

Place the pineapple on its side on a cutting board. Using a sharp knife, cut the fruit crosswise, into ½-inch slices.

Using the tip of a sharp knife, or a small round cookie cutter, remove the pineapple's core.

Next, trim away the rind from the outside of each slice.

Now just flick out the woody eyes with the tip of your knife.

AMBROSIA

Prep **25 MINUTES + CHILLING**

3   oranges, peeled and sectioned

2   small grapefruit, peeled and sectioned

½   cup orange marmalade

1   teaspoon vanilla extract

2   containers (8 ounces each) fat-free lemon yogurt

2   tablespoons sweetened shredded coconut

"Ambrosia" is what the Greek gods ate as they sat atop Mount Olympus. Today, it refers to a fruit dessert, usually with plenty of oranges and other fruits, plus coconut. It's a popular dish served during the holidays throughout the Deep South. Our version adds a hint of vanilla plus lemony yogurt to round out the flavors.

LET'S BEGIN Combine the sectioned fruit in a medium bowl. Gently stir in the marmalade and vanilla, being careful not to break up the sections. Chill for 20 minutes, if you wish.

TOP & SERVE Spoon the fruit into individual serving dishes. Spoon ½ cup of the yogurt over each serving and top with the coconut.

> *Makes 4 servings*
>
> *Per serving: 314 calories, 8g protein, 70g carbohydrates, 1g fat, 1g saturated fat, 0mg cholesterol, 100mg sodium*

SuperQuick
FRUIT TACOS

Prep **20 MINUTES**

5   cups assorted chopped or sliced fresh fruit (apples, bananas, grapes, or strawberries)

2   tablespoons orange juice

12   taco shells, warmed

1   cup (8 ounces) low-fat strawberry yogurt

½   cup toasted coconut (optional)

½   cup sliced almonds (optional)

Who says that tacos have to be stuffed with meat and veggies? Fill them with yogurt and fruit and watch the kids eat them up. They'll never guess how healthy they are!

LET'S BEGIN Combine the fruit and orange juice in a large bowl.

STUFF THEM Fill each taco shell with some of the fruit mixture.

TOP & SERVE Top each taco with the yogurt, coconut, and almonds, if desired.

> *Makes 12 tacos*
>
> *Per taco: 110 calories, 2g protein, 22g carbohydrates, 3g fat, 1g saturated fat, 0mg cholesterol, 103mg sodium*

Ambrosia

KALEIDOSCOPE POPS

Prep **15 MINUTES + FREEZING**

2   cups diced fresh fruit

2   cups apple juice

6   paper cups (6–8 ounces each)

6   popsicle sticks

A popsicle is the ideal way to cool down on a warm—or hot—summer's day and it's low in calories too! No fancy popsicle molds needed here: simple paper cups do the trick.

LET'S BEGIN Spoon the fruit evenly into each cup. Fill the cups evenly with the apple juice. Place the cups on a level surface in the freezer. Freeze until partially frozen and slushy, about 1 hour. Insert a popsicle stick into the center of each pop. Freeze until firm, about 3 hours.

Makes 6 pops

Per pop: 60 calories, 1g protein, 16g carbohydrates, 0g fat, 0g saturated fat, 0mg cholesterol, 0mg sodium

SuperQuick
GRAPES WITH GINGER CREAM

Prep **10 MINUTES + CHILLING**

We love the combination of grapes and ginger. But for a change, you can forget the ginger and instead top the dessert with a generous sprinkling of maple sugar or even maple syrup.

6   cups seedless black or purple grapes

1   tablespoon grated fresh ginger

2   cups low-fat vanilla yogurt

2   tablespoons packed brown sugar

¼   teaspoon cinnamon

Fresh mint leaves for garnish (optional)

LET'S BEGIN Toss the grapes with the ginger in a large bowl. Spoon equal amounts of fruit into 4 stemmed glasses or serving dishes. Carefully spoon ½ cup of the yogurt over the grapes. Sprinkle each serving with ½ tablespoon of the brown sugar followed by a dusting of cinnamon.

CHILL & SERVE Place the desserts in the refrigerator for 20 to 30 minutes or until chilled but not icy cold. Garnish with fresh mint, if desired.

Makes 4 servings

Per serving: 222 calories, 7g protein, 48g carbohydrates, 3g fat, 1g saturated fat, 6mg cholesterol, 84mg sodium

SuperQuick
FRUITY PARFAITS

Prep **10 MINUTES**

2   cups low-fat fruit-
     flavored yogurt

½   cup graham cracker
     crumbs

2   cups diced fresh fruit

2   cups natural applesauce

Fruit-filled parfaits are always a welcome way to end a meal. Here, a light and refreshing combination of diced fresh fruit (of your choice), applesauce, sweet and crunchy graham cracker crumbs, and fruit-flavored yogurt (how about lemon?) make it fast and fabulous.

LET'S BEGIN Spoon ¼ cup of the yogurt into 4 parfait glasses. Sprinkle 1 tablespoon of the graham cracker crumbs over the yogurt. Spoon ¼ cup of the fruit over the crumbs. Top the fruit with ¼ cup of the applesauce. Repeat the layers. Cover and chill until ready to serve.

Makes 4 servings

Per serving: 260 calories, 7g protein, 54g carbohydrates, 3g fat, 1g saturated fat, 5mg cholesterol, 128mg sodium

RASPBERRY TRIFLE

Prep **30 MINUTES + CHILLING**

2 packages (3.4 ounces each) instant vanilla pudding mix

2 pints fresh raspberries

2 jars (10 ounces each) raspberry spreadable fruit

3 packages (3 ounces each) ladyfingers, cut in half lengthwise

In England where trifles originated, they often make this layered pudding dessert with homemade leftover sponge cake, instead of ladyfingers. Before adding the filling, they douse the cake with spirits, such as a nice sherry. Thanks to pudding mix and ladyfingers, our version is much quicker to make than the traditional one—but just as good.

LET'S BEGIN Prepare the pudding mix according to the package directions. Combine the raspberries and spreadable fruit in a bowl, then set aside.

LAYER Arrange half of the ladyfingers along the bottom and sides of a 2½-quart clear glass bowl. Layer half of the pudding and half of the raspberry mixture. Repeat, ending with the raspberry mixture.

CHILL IT Cover and refrigerate until ready to serve.

Makes 10 servings

Per serving: 322 calories, 6g protein, 64g carbohydrates, 5g fat, 2g saturated fat, 101mg cholesterol, 366mg sodium

---

Food Facts

FROM ENGLAND TO AMERICA— THE HISTORY OF THE TRIFLE

Trifles have been enjoyed for many centuries and for good reason. They are festive, delicious, and easy to whip up for a crowd.

The word *trifle* is derived from the Middle English word *truffle*, which is derived from the French word *trufe*

(something of little importance).

The first known printed recipe for a trifle appeared in 1596, but it was little more than spiced cream. By the mid-eighteenth century, however, trifles resembling modern-day versions began appearing.

Biscuits dipped into wine were placed in the bottom of a bowl and custard was poured over them. Eventually the traditional topping of whipped cream took its rightful place and has remained a constant ever since.

Chocolate Quesadillas, page 65

Sweets for the Kids

Kids naturally seem to have a sweet tooth—so we've made this collection just for them! Many of our recipes will bring a smile to young faces just because of their names, such as Wacky Waffles, Dirt Cake, and Chocolate Nugget Critters. Others are tried-and-true kids' favorites, such as our ice cream sundaes, peanut butter fudge, and those delicious camping treats called S'mores. All are kid-friendly, kid-safe, and perfect for little hands to make. Let them top ice cream cones their own way one day, then help them make popcorn balls or cool candies in the microwave another time. They're all quick-fixing, no-bake, fun to create, and—most of all—fun for all to eat!

SNICKERDOODLE ICE CREAM

Prep **10 MINUTES + FREEZING**

½   cup granulated sugar

½   cup packed light brown
     sugar

½   teaspoon cinnamon

⅛   teaspoon nutmeg

2   cups whipping cream

1½ cups half-and-half,
     regular or fat free

1½ teaspoons vanilla extract

The name "snickerdoodle" originated in New England in the 1800s. The funny sounding word has no particular meaning, but is usually associated with a simple cookie flavored with nutmeg and cinnamon. Historians sometimes credit the name to the fact that cooks in New England often gave dishes fun, frolicking, and nonsensical names.

LET'S BEGIN Combine the granulated sugar, brown sugar, cinnamon, and nutmeg in a medium bowl. Stir in the whipping cream, half-and-half, and vanilla.

FREEZE IT Pour the cream mixture into a 1-quart ice cream freezer. Freeze according to the manufacturer's directions for 40 to 60 minutes. Garnish with thin slices of red apple, if desired.

Makes 8 servings

Per serving: 400 calories, 1g protein, 28g carbohydrates, 29g fat, 17g saturated fat, 115mg cholesterol, 45mg sodium

Cook to Cook

WHAT ARE SOME FUN WAYS TO TOP ICE CREAM CONES?

"*Half of the fun of eating an ice cream cone* is licking off, biting off, or chewing off the sweet and lovely things that can top ice cream. The extra munch or crunch the fun-filled toppers provide makes eating a cone that much sweeter—and yummy!

Ice cream toppers come in many guises: think chopped nuts, sprinkles (chocolate or otherwise), toasted coconut, miniature chocolate chips, coarsely crushed cookies, crushed candies (peppermint, butterscotch, or fruity), or melted semisweet, bittersweet, milk, or white chocolate.

Put each of your toppings of choice into a separate soup bowl. Be sure to fill each about halfway. Firmly scoop ice cream into a cone, making sure it will not fall out. *Turn the cone upside down and swirl back and forth into a topping until well coated.* Now get ready to make your mouth happy and your tongue sing!"

BANANA POPS

Prep **12 MINUTES + FREEZING**

1   ripe, medium banana

1½   cups orange banana juice

½   cup sugar

¼   cup unsweetened cocoa

1   can (5 ounces)
       evaporated milk

6   paper cold drink cups
       (5 ounces each)

6   wooden popsicle sticks

Mix banana and chocolate together and you're guaranteed to have a winner. A blender makes speedy work of the pop base—with little cleanup. Popsicle sticks can be found in craft stores, cake decorating stores, and in some kitchenware catalogs.

LET'S BEGIN Slice the banana into a blender container and add the juice. Cover and blend until smooth. Add the sugar and cocoa, then cover again and blend well. Add the evaporated milk, cover, and blend.

POUR & FREEZE Pour the mixture into the paper cups. Freeze about 1 hour, then insert popsicle sticks into the fudge pops. Return the pops to the freezer until firm, about 2 hours. To serve, peel off paper cups.

Makes 6 pops
Per pop: 150 calories, 2g protein, 29g carbohydrates, 2g fat, 1g saturated fat, 2mg cholesterol, 6mg sodium

SuperQuick
ROCKY ROAD SUNDAE

Prep **5 MINUTES**   *Microwave* **1 MINUTE**

1   package (11 ounces)
     peanut butter and
     milk chocolate chips

½   cup whipping cream

2   tablespoons light corn
     syrup

1   teaspoon vanilla
     extract

Attention peanut butter and chocolate lovers! This decadent sauce will turn any ice cream into your favorite flavor.

FIX IT FAST Stir together the first 3 ingredients in a medium microwave-safe bowl. Microwave on High for 1 minute and stir until the chips are melted and the mixture is smooth. If necessary, microwave for an additional 30 seconds at a time, just until smooth when stirred. Stir in the vanilla. Serve the warm topping over ice cream.

Makes 8 sundaes (1 cup ice cream + 3 tablespoons topping each)

Per sundae: 540 calories, 10g protein, 56g carbohydrates, 31g fat, 21g saturated fat, 82mg cholesterol, 176mg sodium

---

Time Savers

MAKING FAST FRUIT POPS

Fruit pops are a great way to cool off on a hot summer's day. Here are a few of our most favorite ones.

   Tip: Fruit pops can be frozen in 3-ounce paper cups, paper cooler cups, popsicle molds, or tartlet pans. Once filled and placed in the freezer, insert wooden sticks after the pops are semi-frozen, which will take about 1½ hours.

ORANGE CREAMSICLE POPS Divide about ½ cup slightly softened orange sherbet among

6 cups. Top with about 1 cup vanilla ice cream and another ½ cup sherbet. Freeze.

RASPBERRY MELON POPS Thaw and puree a package of frozen sweetened raspberries in syrup. Spoon in enough puree to fill the cups halfway. Freeze until partially frozen. Puree about 1½ cups ripe cantaloupe or honeydew in a food processor. Spoon over the raspberry mixture. Freeze.

LEMONADE POPS Fill paper cups with prepared lemonade. Freeze.

WATERMELON-LIME POPS Puree about 3 cups of chunked seedless red watermelon. Add fresh lime juice to taste. Spoon into the cups and freeze.

POLKA DOT YOGURT POPS Gently fold fresh raspberries, blueberries, or halved small strawberries into slightly softened frozen vanilla yogurt. Divide among the cups and freeze.

SuperQuick
POLKA DOT POPCORN BALLS

Prep **10 MINUTES**   Cook **4 MINUTES**

Everyone loves popcorn for snacking, especially when friends come by. Turn the event into a party by letting the group help make these dotted popcorn balls. Hint: Dried cranberries are the dots, which makes them perfect for holiday time.

8	cups plain popcorn (unbuttered and unsalted)
1	cup sweetened dried cranberries
½	cup firmly packed brown sugar
½	cup pure maple syrup
3	tablespoons butter or margarine

LET'S BEGIN Combine the popcorn and cranberries in a large mixing bowl and set aside. Combine the remaining ingredients in a small saucepan. Stir over medium heat until the butter melts and the mixture comes to a boil and thickens slightly, about 4 minutes. Pour the mixture over the popcorn and cranberries, stirring until coated.

SHAPE & COOL Dip your hands in cold water, then shape the popcorn mixture into 2-inch balls, pressing together firmly to hold their shape. Place the balls on waxed paper and let cool completely. Let stand overnight to harden. Wrap in decorative plastic wrap, if desired.

Makes 12 servings

Per serving: 153 calories, 1g protein, 31g carbohydrates, 3g fat, 2g saturated fat, 8mg cholesterol, 36mg sodium

LUNCHBOX PEANUT BUTTER TREATS

Prep **5 MINUTES**   *Cook* **10 MINUTES + COOLING**

¼   cup butter or
     margarine

30   marshmallows or
     3 cups miniature
     marshmallows

⅓   cup light corn syrup

1⅓   cups peanut butter
     chips

5   cups crisp rice cereal

Calling all lunchbox toters! These quick-cook treats are fun to make and fun to eat. Invite some friends home after school and have a ball! Don't forget to stir up a double batch so your friends can take some home.

LET'S BEGIN Melt the butter in a large saucepan over low heat. Stir the marshmallows into the melted butter. Cook, stirring constantly, until the marshmallows melt completely. Remove the saucepan from the heat and stir in the corn syrup. Add the peanut butter chips and stir until chips are melted and mixture is smooth.

PRESS & CUT Immediately stir in the cereal until it's well coated. Press the mixture into a greased 9-inch square baking pan. Cool completely, then cut into bars. Store in an airtight container in a cool place.

Makes about 16 bars

Per bar: 225 calories, 5g protein, 33g carbohydrates, 8g fat, 7g saturated fat, 8mg cholesterol, 167mg sodium

SNACKING BLOCKS

Prep **10 MINUTES + CHILLING**

4   envelopes unflavored gelatin

½   cup cold water

2   cups orange juice, heated to boiling

1½   cups strawberry-flavored syrup

These jiggly-wiggly fruit-flavored gelatin blocks will give kids a laugh—and a good dose of vitamin C. Make them even more fun by cutting into shapes with cookie cutters.

LET'S BEGIN Sprinkle the gelatin over the water in a large bowl and let stand for 5 minutes to soften. Add the juice and stir until the gelatin is completely dissolved. Stir in the syrup.

CHILL & SERVE Pour the mixture into a 13 × 9-inch pan and refrigerate for 4 hours or until firm. Cut into blocks or into shapes using cookie cutters.

Makes 36 blocks

Per block: 42 calories, 1g protein, 10g carbohydrates, 0g fat, 0g saturated fat, 0mg cholesterol, 5mg sodium

---

Food Facts

WHOOPIE FOR WHOOPIE PIES!

These fun treats called Whoopie Pies are not pies at all. They're really two large chocolate cookies (so soft that they're more like cake) that are "glued" together with fluffy white filling. As the tale goes, these pies were baked by mothers in the Pennsylvania Dutch countryside who liked to make cookie treats for their kids from leftover cake batter. Just where the name comes from is not well known. It might have evolved from the "whoop of joy" that came upon the children's faces when they were offered such a great treat.

In the Tennessee town of Chattanooga, bakers have been baking something similar since 1917. There, two giant-size chocolate cookies are sandwiched together with marshmallow filling, then covered with chocolate.

Kids love these cookies, which they say are as big as the moon. And that's the reason they're affectionately call moon pies!

WAKE 'EM UP WACKY WAFFLES
Prep **15 MINUTES**   *Cook* **15 MINUTES**

1½   **cups buttermilk baking mix**

1   **cup buttermilk**

1   **large egg**

1   **tablespoon vegetable oil**

½   **cup milk chocolate candies**

Confectioners' sugar

Maple syrup

They're wicky, they're wacky, they're wonderful! They're fast homemade Belgian waffles with chocolate melted inside. What a foolproof, fun way to get kids to eat their breakfast.

LET'S BEGIN Preheat your Belgian waffle iron according to the manufacturer's directions. Whisk the baking mix, buttermilk, egg, and oil together until well mixed.

SPOON & SPRINKLE Spoon about ½ cup batter into hot waffle iron. Sprinkle with about 2 tablespoons candies and drizzle on about ½ cup more batter.

COOK Close lid and bake until steaming stops, according to your manufacturer's instructions. Repeat with the remaining batter. Sprinkle with the sugar and serve immediately with the syrup (warm it first if you wish).

CHOCOLATE WAFFLES

Substitute 1¼ cups biscuit baking mix, ¼ cup unsweetened cocoa powder, and ½ cup sugar for the 2 cups biscuit baking mix. Prepare and cook as directed above.

Makes 5 Belgian waffles
Per waffle: 528 calories, 7g protein, 95g carbohydrates, 14g fat, 5g saturated fat, 47mg cholesterol, 549mg sodium

TINY LOVE CAKES

Prep **45 MINUTES + MICROWAVING + CHILLING**

1   (16 ounce) frozen pound
    cake, thawed

1   (16 ounce) can prepared
    vanilla frosting

Red food coloring

1   tube chocolate
    decorative frosting, with
    plain tip

1   (14 ounce) bag milk
    chocolate candies for
    Valentine's Day

Who could resist these adorable Valentine's Day cakes? And to think you made them yourself! Share them with friends, family, and your very own true love.

LET'S BEGIN Line a cookie sheet with waxed paper and place a wire cooling rack on top. Set aside. Cut the pound cake lengthwise into 9 slices, each about 1 inch thick. Using a heart-shaped cookie cutter (2 to 2¼ inches), cut out 2 heart shapes per cake slice. (Save trimmings for another use, such as trifles, rum balls, or snacking.) Place the heart-shaped cake pieces on the wire cooling rack.

FROST & CHILL Spoon ¼ cup of the vanilla frosting into a resealable plastic bag and set aside. Using the red food coloring, tint the remaining frosting a light pink, and spoon it into a glass measuring cup. Microwave the pink frosting on Medium for 5 to 10 seconds, or until pourable (do not overheat!). Pour the pink frosting over the heart-shaped cake pieces, to cover both the tops and the sides, reusing the drippings and reheating if necessary. Refrigerate until set, about 30 minutes.

DECORATE Using scissors, snip a small corner from the resealable plastic bag filled with the white frosting, and use it to pipe designs on the tops and sides of the heart-shaped cake pieces. Attach candies in different designs, then pipe messages on the tops with the decorative chocolate frosting.

Makes 18 cakes
Per cake: 345 calories, 3g protein, 47g carbohydrates, 16g fat, 7g saturated fat, 61mg cholesterol, 186mg sodium

CHOCOLATE QUESADILLAS
Prep **10 MINUTES**   *Cook* **3 MINUTES**

4   flour tortillas
     (7 to 8 inches each)

¼   cup creamy or crunchy
     peanut butter

¼   cup marshmallow cream

2   small bananas, sliced

½   cup milk chocolate or
     semisweet chocolate
     chips

Take a trip with your kids and their friends down south of the border where the living is easy, colorful, and fun. Bring back their favorite tortillas and turn them into dessert. You'll think you've just landed in Mexico on holiday!

LET'S BEGIN Lightly coat one side of each tortilla with cooking spray. Place the tortillas on a clean work surface with the coated sides down.

SPREAD & FOLD Spread 1 tablespoon of peanut butter and 1 tablespoon marshmallow cream on half of each tortilla. Arrange ¼ of the banana slices and 2 tablespoons of the chocolate chips over marshmallow cream. Fold each tortilla over to cover the filling.

BROWN & SERVE Heat a large nonstick skillet over medium heat for 1 minute. Add 2 quesadillas and cook for 1 to 2 minutes or until tortillas are golden brown and crisp. Turn once during cooking. Repeat with remaining quesadillas. Serve warm.

Makes 4 servings
Per serving: 548 calories, 11g protein, 80g carbohydrates, 21g fat, 7g saturated fat, 5mg cholesterol, 350mg sodium

MICROWAVE PEANUT BUTTER FUDGE

Prep **15 MINUTES**   *Microwave* **3 MINUTES + CHILLING**

⅔   cup butter or margarine

⅔   cup chunky-style peanut butter

6   cups confectioners' sugar

⅓   cup milk

1   tablespoon vanilla extract

What, no chocolate? You'll never miss it! These pea-nutty squares make a delicious anytime snack or smart dessert, and they're guaranteed to satisfy any sweet tooth.

LET'S BEGIN Place the butter and peanut butter in a large microwaveable bowl. Microwave on High until the butter melts (1½ to 2 minutes). Stir with a wooden spoon until well mixed, then stir in the remaining ingredients until lumps of sugar disappear. Microwave on High until softened but not bubbly (1 to 1½ minutes). Stir.

CHILL & CUT Pour into a buttered 8-inch square baking pan. Cover and refrigerate for 1 hour or until firm. Cut into squares. Store in the refrigerator.

Makes 3 dozen pieces

Per piece: 140 calories, 1g protein, 21g carbohydrates, 6g fat, 2g saturated fat, 10mg cholesterol, 50mg sodium

SuperQuick
CHOCOLATE NUGGETS CRITTERS

Prep **5 MINUTES**   *Microwave* **30 SECONDS**

2	bite-size nugget-shaped chocolate candies
2	chocolate wafer cookies
2	large marshmallows
8	whole almonds
2	pecan halves

Kids will love creating these cute little critters. Be sure to supervise them while they use the microwave to soften the marshmallows.

LET'S BEGIN Remove the wrappers from chocolate candies. Place the chocolate cookies on a paper towel, top with the marshmallows, and microwave on High for 10 seconds or until the marshmallows puff.

FINAL TOUCH Press a chocolate candy into the center of each marshmallow. Press 4 almonds, as feet, and pecan halves, as heads, onto each marshmallow.

Makes 2 servings

Per serving: 130 calories, 3g protein, 13g carbohydrates, 8g fat, 1g saturated fat, 1mg cholesterol, 42mg sodium

---

Microwave in Minutes

COOL-COOK SWEETS

When little hands are involved with cooking, the microwave can be a "kitchen helper made in heaven." Naturally, there no dangerous flames to worry about, but food does get steaming hot, so safety steps are all important. Here, a few microwave sweets to keep kids busy and having fun safely in the kitchen:

POPCORN BALLS Buy the regular microwave popcorn without any seasoning and pop according to directions (you should have about 2 quarts). Place in a large bowl. Melt about 30 caramels with 2 tablespoons water in a microwave-safe bowl. Microwave on High for 2 to 3 minutes until melted. Pour over popcorn and toss to coat. When cool enough to handle, have kids butter their hands, then make lot of caramel popcorn balls.

FAST FUDGE This one's easy-does-it! Combine two packages (the 12-ounce size) of chocolate chips with a can of sweetened condensed milk (the 14-ounce size) in a microwave-safe bowl. Then let the kids heat it a little for a few seconds, stir a little, and on and on until the mixture is melted and smooth. Spread out in a jellyroll pan, let them sprinkle it with some chopped nuts, then cool and cut. And fudge is ready—easy as 1, 2, 3!

"Make Mine Chocolate" Waffles

Prep **10 minutes**   *Cook* **18 minutes**

¾ cup all-purpose flour

½ cup sugar

1 tablespoon unsweetened cocoa

2 teaspoons baking powder

½ cup no-fat sour cream

½ cup skim milk

¼ cup butter or margarine, melted

1 large egg

1 teaspoon vanilla extract

1 pint low-fat vanilla frozen yogurt or ice milk

2 cups hulled and sliced fresh strawberries

Who says sundaes have to be served in a bowl? These are stacked up on scrumptious chocolate waffles, crowned with yogurt or ice cream if you like, then topped with fresh berries.

LET'S BEGIN Heat the waffle iron to medium-high heat according to the manufacturer's directions. In a large bowl combine the flour, sugar, cocoa, and baking powder. In a medium bowl stir together the sour cream, milk, butter, egg, and vanilla until smooth. Stir the sour cream mixture into the flour mixture until well blended.

BROWN & SERVE Pour about 2 tablespoons of the batter onto the center of each section of the waffle iron. Cook for 3 to 4 minutes, or until waffles stop steaming. Repeat with remaining batter. To serve, place each waffle on a serving plate. Top with a scoop of frozen yogurt and strawberries. Sprinkle with confectioners' sugar, if desired.

Makes 6 servings

Per serving: 325 calories, 7g protein, 48g carbohydrates, 12g fat, 6g saturated fat, 60mg cholesterol, 231mg sodium

TORTILLAS FANTASTICAS
Prep **5 MINUTES**   *Cook* **5 MINUTES**

1   can (1 pound 5 ounces)
      cherry pie filling,
      divided

4   flour tortillas

¾   cup slivered almonds

½   cup vegetable oil

¼   cup confectioners' sugar

Chocolate curls, if desired

What fun—stuffing tortillas with cherries instead of meat! Let the kids help; they'll love the folding and the rolling—and especially the eating.

LET'S BEGIN Reserve ¼ cup of the pie filling for the topping. Spoon the remainder onto the center of each tortilla. Sprinkle 2 tablespoons of the almonds over the pie filling. Fold in two sides of each tortilla and roll tortillas around the filling.

SIZZLE & SERVE Pour enough oil into a large skillet to measure ¼ inch. Heat over medium-high heat until the oil sizzles when the edge of a tortilla is dipped in it. Place 2 tortillas seam-side down in the skillet. Fry about 1 minute on each side or until golden and crispy. Drain briefly on paper towels. Place the tortilla on individual dessert plates and sprinkle or sieve confectioners' sugar over the top. Spoon the pie filling over each serving, then sprinkle the remaining ¼ cup almonds and chocolate curls. Serve hot.

Makes 4 servings

Per serving: 618 calories, 12g protein, 95g carbohydrates, 22g fat, 3g saturated fat, 0mg cholesterol, 371mg sodium

SuperQuick
BUTTERSCOTCH FUDGE CUT-OUTS

Prep **10 MINUTES**   *Microwave* **2 MINUTES + COOLING**

2   packages (11 ounces each) butterscotch chips

1   can (14 ounces) sweetened condensed milk (not evaporated milk)

What a simple, foolproof way to make fudge—2 ingredients, 2 micro-waving minutes, and little hands to help cut it out in fun shapes.

LET'S BEGIN Line a 15½ × 10½ × 1-inch jelly-roll pan with foil and set aside. Combine the butterscotch chips and sweet-ened condensed milk in a large microwaveable bowl. Micro-wave on High (100%) for 1 minute, then stir. Continue heating 15 seconds at a time, or until mixture is smooth when stirred.

COOL & CUT Immediately spread the mixture evenly into the prepared pan. Cover and refrigerate until firm, about 10 minutes. Use the foil to lift fudge out of the pan. Place the fudge on a cutting board and peel off foil. Use small cookie cutters to cut out your favorite shapes.

> **Makes 2 pounds fudge (32 cut-outs/1 ounce each)**
> *Per serving: 173 calories, 1g protein, 23g carbohydrates, 8g fat, 7g saturated fat, 4mg cholesterol, 41mg sodium*

SuperQuick
DIRT CAKE

Prep **15 MINUTES**

1   package (about 5.9 ounces) instant chocolate pudding and pie filling mix

3   cups cold milk

1   cup chocolate cookie crumbs, about 45 to 50 crushed chocolate wafers

⅔   cup chocolate syrup

1   container (8 ounces) frozen whipped topping, thawed

1   package (3 ounces) gummy worms

With three different kinds of chocolate, this cake really does look like dirt! Add gummy worms for that next party.

LET'S BEGIN Prepare the chocolate pudding according to the package directions using the 3 cups milk. Combine the cookie crumbs and chocolate syrup in a medium bowl. Set aside ¼ cup of the crumb mixture.

LAYER IT Press half of the remaining crumb mixture into a 9-inch square dish or pan. Spoon half the pudding over the crumbs, then spoon half the whipped topping over the pud-ding. Repeat the layers. Sprinkle with reserved crumbs and top with the gummy worms. To serve, spoon into serving dishes.

> **Makes 8 servings**
> *Per serving: 445 calories, 6g protein, 75g carbohydrates, 12g fat, 8g saturated fat, 12g cholesterol, 575mg sodium*

SuperQuick
PEANUT BUTTER S'MORES

Prep **15 MINUTES + MICROWAVING**

18	graham cracker squares
3	tablespoons creamy peanut butter
7	chocolate sandwich cookies, coarsely chopped (about ⅔ cup)
3	tablespoons hot fudge dessert topping
½	cup miniature marshmallows

Maybe these aren't quite as much fun as cooking 'em over an outdoor fire, but they taste surprisingly similar. And they're really, really fast and fun!

LET'S BEGIN Spread 9 of the crackers with peanut butter, about 1 teaspoon for each cracker. Top with 1 tablespoon of the chopped cookies, 1 teaspoon fudge sauce, and 3 to 4 marshmallows. Place the remaining crackers on top to form a sandwich.

MELT & SERVE Place 4 or 5 sandwiches on a microwaveable plate. Microwave on High for 10 to 15 seconds or until marshmallows begin to melt. Repeat with the remaining sandwiches. Serve warm.

Makes 9 sandwiches

Per sandwich: 140 calories, 3g protein, 19g carbohydrates, 6g fat, 1g saturated fat, 0mg cholesterol, 161mg sodium

Cooking Basics

MAKING FAST TREATS WITH KIDS

Put a smile on a kid's face: Let them help make—and then enjoy—a super-easy, super-tasty homemade ice cream treat.

FUN SKEWERS Thread regular-size marshmallows, chunks of banana, and small whole strawberries onto bamboo skewers. Serve with fudge sauce for dipping.

ICE CREAM BALLS Turn a favorite cookie, such as peanut butter, oatmeal, or chocolate chip, into

coarse crumbs in a food processor. Put into a shallow soup bowl. Place scoops of a complementary ice cream on a foil-lined cookie sheet and freeze until very firm. Quickly roll each scoop in the cookie crumbs and return to the freezer. Serve with caramel or fudge sauce.

ICE CREAM CONES YOUR WAY Melt some chocolate in the microwave and paint it on the outside of waffle ice cream cones. Roll

the cones in sprinkles, chopped nuts, crushed peppermint candies, or heath bar bits. Set aside until the chocolate sets, then fill with ice cream.

THE WORKS Personalize vanilla, chocolate, or strawberry ice cream by letting it soften slightly in the refrigerator, then folding in nuts, M&M's, chocolate chips, coarsely crushed cookies, brownie bits, miniature marshmallows, or candied cherries.

CIRCUS PIE

Prep **30 MINUTES + FREEZING**

The circus is in town—or soon will be! Assemble this ice cream pie in mere minutes from a prepared crust and your favorite ice cream. Then let the kids help you build the circus tent on top of the pie. Such fun!

1   (9-inch) ready-made graham cracker piecrust

½   gallon ice cream (your favorite flavor)

2   containers (8 ounces each) whipped topping

12   ice cream cones

Ready-made frosting (assorted colors)

Construction paper

Toothpicks

Clear tape

LET'S BEGIN Fill the crust with ice cream, smoothing it with a warm spatula. Pipe or spoon whipped topping on top of the pie.

DECORATE Make the ice cream cones into circus tents and clowns using the colored frosting. Cut out small triangles from construction paper to make flags for the tops of the tents. Fasten them to a toothpick with tape, then place flags on top of the cones.

TOP & FREEZE Place the cones on top of the ice cream pie.

Makes 8 servings
Per serving: 665 calories, 7g protein, 82g carbohydrates, 32g fat, 20g saturated fat, 58mg cholesterol, 325mg sodium

Coconut Fudge Bars, page 78

Chill It!

Yes, you really can serve a beautiful Key Lime Pie just like they do down in the Florida Keys—without ever turning on the oven. Just pick up a few ingredients including a crumb crust, whip up the filling in minutes, and chill it. That's all it takes to impress your guests with fabulous pie, our Quick Cook way. Master an impressive soufflé, a heavenly chocolate mousse, or even an Italian Tiramisu in little time. Then relax, knowing that dessert's in the fridge or the freezer, just waiting for dinner. Also, check out our tips for cutting the chilling time and our foolproof secrets for melting chocolate. They're all part of our no-bake, sure-hit way to serve dessert.

STRAWBERRY CHIFFON PIE

Prep **20 MINUTES + COOLING**

½   cup water at room temperature

1   envelope (7 grams) unflavored gelatin

1   package (10 ounces) frozen sweetened strawberries, thawed, drained, juice reserved

¼   cup granulated sugar

1   tablespoon all-purpose flour

3   tablespoons fresh lemon juice

⅓   cup ice water

⅓   cup nonfat dry milk

2   tablespoons granulated sugar

1   prebaked 9-inch (4-cup volume) deep-dish pie crust

Chiffon is usually a fluffy pie-filling mixture that needs beaten egg whites to become airy. Here nonfat dry milk whipped with ice water achieves the same thing—but oh so easily!

FREEZE Put small mixer bowl and beaters in freezer to chill. Pour ½ cup water into small bowl; sprinkle with gelatin.

COMBINE Combine ¼ cup sugar and flour in small saucepan. Add strawberry juice and gelatin mixture; mix well. Cook over low heat, stirring frequently, until sugar is dissolved. Remove from heat. Stir in strawberries and 2 tablespoons lemon juice. Pour into large mixer bowl. Refrigerate for 20 minutes or until thick and syrupy, but not set.

BEAT Beat ice water and dry milk in chilled bowl for 3 to 4 minutes or until soft peaks form. Add remaining lemon juice and beat for 3 to 4 minutes or until stiff. Fold in 2 tablespoons sugar; blend on low speed. With wire whisk, mix whipped topping into strawberry mixture. Pour into pie crust. Refrigerate for 2 hours or until firm.

Makes 8 servings
Per serving: 206 calories, 4g protein, 32g carbohydrates, 8g fat, 2g saturated fat, 1mg cholesterol, 141mg sodium

---

Time Savers

CHILL IT FASTER

Here's our quick and easy way to cool down custard, pudding, fruit sauces, or ice cream bases. Pour the still warm or hot mixture into a bowl and set into a larger bowl that contains very cold water and a generous amount of ice. Now chill it completely in one of two ways: place custard in the refrigerator and take it out occasionally to stir, so the whole mixture cools down evenly. Or leave it on the counter and stir every 5 minutes or so until the mixture cools throughout. Consistent stirring will prevent a skin from forming on egg-based mixtures.

STRAWBERRY-CHOCOLATE MOUSSE PARFAIT

Prep **30 MINUTES + CHILLING**

1   cup (about 5 ounces) chocolate cookie or chocolate graham cracker crumbs

3   tablespoons butter or margarine, melted

2   pints strawberries, stemmed and halved

2   cups (12 ounces) semisweet chocolate morsels

½   cup water

2   tablespoons light corn syrup

2½ cups cold whipping cream

1   tablespoon sugar

Chocolate and strawberries are an inspired combination! The refrigerator does most of the work in this magical cake. Once the mousse is set, it's ready to serve—and impress!

LET'S BEGIN In a small bowl, blend the crumbs and butter thoroughly. Press evenly onto the bottom of a 9-inch springform pan. Stand strawberry halves, touching, side-by-side, pointed ends up with cut sides against the side of the pan. Set aside.

MIX & CHILL Place the chocolate in the container of an electric blender. In a small saucepan over medium heat, combine the water and corn syrup. Bring the mixture to a boil and simmer for 1 minute. Immediately pour the hot syrup over the chocolate. Cover and blend until smooth. Cool to room temperature. Meanwhile, in large mixing bowl, beat 1½ cups of the cream to form stiff peaks. With a rubber spatula, gently fold the cooled chocolate mixture into the whipped cream to blend thoroughly. Pour into the prepared pan and level the surface. (Points of strawberries might extend above chocolate mixture.) Cover and refrigerate for 4 to 24 hours.

FINAL TOUCH Up to 2 hours before serving, in a medium mixer bowl, beat the remaining 1 cup of cream to form soft peaks. Add the sugar and beat to form stiff peaks. Remove the side of the pan and place the cake on a flat serving plate. Pipe or dollop whipped cream onto the top of the cake. Arrange the remaining halved strawberries over the cake. To serve, cut into wedges with a thin-bladed knife, wiping the blade with a dampened paper towel between cuts.

> *Makes 12 servings*
> *Per serving: 406 calories, 5g protein, 36g carbohydrates, 30g fat, 19g saturated fat, 76mg cholesterol, 153mg sodium*

Coconut Fudge Bars

Prep **20 MINUTES**   *Cook* **10 MINUTES + CHILLING**

1   cup (2 sticks) butter or margarine, melted

2½   cups graham cracker crumbs

1   cup sugar

1   can (5 ounces) evaporated milk (about ⅔ cup)

1   package (10½ ounces) miniature marshmallows

1   package (12 ounces) semisweet chocolate chunks (about 2 cups)

1   cup walnuts, chopped

1   cup flaked coconut, toasted

These lusciously layered bar cookies will disappear as fast as you cut them.

LET'S BEGIN Mix ¾ cup of the melted butter and crumbs in a medium bowl. Press the crumbs onto the bottom of a foil-lined 13 × 9-inch pan. Set aside.

LAYER IT In a large saucepan, combine the remaining ¼ cup butter, sugar, evaporated milk, and marshmallows. Stir over medium heat until the mixture comes to a boil. Boil for 5 minutes, stirring constantly. Add the chocolate and cook, stirring frequently, until the chocolate is completely melted. Immediately pour the hot chocolate mixture over the crumb crust. Spread to coat the crust evenly. Sprinkle with the walnuts and coconut, pressing lightly into the chocolate layer.

CHILL & CUT Refrigerate for 2 hours or until firm. Cut into bars. Store in an airtight container in the refrigerator.

Makes 32 bars
Per bar: 211 calories, 2g protein, 24g carbohydrates, 13g fat, 6g saturated fat, 17mg cholesterol, 81mg sodium

BUTTERSCOTCH PUDDING

Prep **20 MINUTES**   *Microwave* **5 MINUTES + CHILLING**

½   cup firmly packed brown
     sugar

2   tablespoons cornstarch

¼   teaspoon salt

1⅔ cups milk

1   egg yolk, lightly beaten

3   tablespoons butter

1   teaspoon vanilla extract

Got 20 minutes? If the answer is yes, this fantastic homemade butterscotch pudding is for you. It is prepared with ease in the microwave.

LET'S BEGIN Combine the brown sugar, cornstarch, and salt in a 1-quart glass measuring cup. Stir in the milk. Microwave, uncovered, on High for 4 to 5 minutes or until thickened and bubbly, stirring after every minute. Stir about ½ cup of the hot mixture into the egg yolk in a small bowl. Return the egg mixture to the measuring cup, stirring to mix well. Microwave, uncovered, on High for 30 seconds or until bubbly.

MIX & CHILL Stir in the butter and vanilla until butter is melted. Cover the surface with plastic wrap. Chill for 1 hour. Pour the mixture into 4 dessert dishes and chill until serving time.

Makes 4 servings

Per serving: 277 calories, 4g protein, 35g carbohydrates, 14g fat, 7g saturated fat, 86mg cholesterol, 267mg sodium

Cooking Basics

THE PERFECT PUDDING

A satiny smooth, rich pudding is guaranteed to bring smiles to all those around your dinner table. Making a perfect homemade pudding is easier than you might think. The most popular puddings are chocolate, vanilla, and butterscotch. These creamy desserts are simply a mixture of milk, sugar, cornstarch, and flavoring. Here's what to keep in mind when making them:

NO LUMPS, PLEASE! The job of the cornstarch is to bind and thicken the pudding ingredients into a lovely, smooth pudding.

To avoid lumping, use a heavy-bottomed saucepan, which provides heat that is both even and gentle. Stir your pudding with a heat-safe rubber spatula, which can easily reach the bottom, side, and corners, so you are assured of stirring all of the mixture as it cooks. In most recipes, the cornstarch is first added to a small amount of liquid, creating a runny paste. This is another way to ensure a lump-less pudding.

Once the pudding is thick and bubbling, pour into one large or several small dishes—the choice is yours. If you like your pudding with a skin on top, just leave it alone. But, if you prefer your pudding without, press a piece of plastic wrap directly onto the surface of the warm pudding. Once the pudding is totally cooled, remove it.

The last step in serving the perfect pudding is to pass a bowl of slightly sweetened, softly whipped cream. Ah, perfection!

COOL 'N' CREAMY CHOCOLATE PIE

Prep **20 MINUTES + FREEZING**

1   package (3 ounces)
      cream cheese, softened

¼   cup sugar

1   teaspoon vanilla extract

½   cup chocolate syrup

1   cup (½ pint) cold
      whipping cream

1   package (6 ounces)
      crumb pie crust

Sliced fresh fruit (optional)

Chocolate curls (optional)

Chocolate syrup adds tons of real chocolate flavor without having to chop and melt. Saves you lots of prep time! Give the cream cheese time to soften before you beat it or it will have small lumps. Tip: Cream cheese can be softened in the microwave on Low for a few seconds—keep an eye on it.

LET'S BEGIN Beat the cream cheese, sugar, and vanilla in a medium bowl until blended. Gradually add the syrup, beating until smooth. Beat the whipping cream until stiff. Carefully fold into the chocolate mixture. Pour into the crust. Cover and freeze until firm, about 3 hours.

FINAL TOUCH Just before serving, garnish the pie with fruit and chocolate curls, if desired.

Makes 6 servings

Per serving: 436 calories, 4g protein, 45g carbohydrates, 26g fat, 14g saturated fat, 70mg cholesterol, 256mg sodium

---

Cooking Basics

UNMOLDING A DESSERT

Is there a kitchen task more stressful than unmolding a dessert while guests patiently wait? Here is our stress-free method—we promise!

To unmold a gelatin-based dessert, set a large bowl of very warm (not hot) water on the counter. Rinse your serving plate with very cold water, shake off the excess, and place it on the counter. Run the tip of a small knife around the edge of the dessert. Lower the mold halfway into the water and hold it there for 5 seconds. Lift it out and shake it back and forth; see if the dessert moves at all. If not, lower it into water again. Place the serving plate, upside down, on top of the mold. Hold the mold and plate together, quickly invert them, and place on the counter. Gently shake the mold: the dessert should drop onto the plate. If not, shake it again. Lift off the mold. Voilà!

To unmold custard-type desserts (panna cotta or caramel custards), run the tip of a small knife around the edges of the custards. Invert them onto dessert plates. Hold a cup and plate together and shake somewhat vigorously until the custard falls out. Sometimes you have to shake the custard several times.

On the Menu

Here's what people in the various regions across America treat themselves to when they're craving a chilled sweet treat.

NORTHEAST
Lemon Water Ice
Cranberry Sherbet
Apple Snow with Custard Sauce

SOUTH
Banana Pudding
Lemon Fluff
Frozen Orange Sherbet-Filled Oranges

MIDWEST
Frozen Pumpkin Pie
Buttermilk Sherbet
Ozark Bread Pudding

WEST
California Citrus Chiffon Pie
Orange Soufflés
New Mexican Flan

CHILLED ORANGE SOUFFLÉ

Prep **10 MINUTES**   *Cook* **10 MINUTES + CHILLING**

Yes, it's true that this ethereal, light-as-a-feather orange soufflé needs a good 6 hours to firm up. The good news is that this is the perfect dessert to prepare in the morning—or even a day ahead. Remember eggs are easiest to separate when they're cold from the fridge.

1	envelope unflavored gelatin
¾	cup sugar
3	large egg yolks, slightly beaten
1	tablespoon finely shredded orange peel
½	cup orange juice
⅓	cup water
3	large egg whites, at room temperature
1	cup cold whipping cream

Orange peel, cut into long, thin strips (optional)

LET'S BEGIN Stir together the gelatin and sugar in a medium saucepan and set aside. Combine the egg yolks, shredded orange peel, orange juice, and water in a small mixing bowl. Stir the orange mixture into the gelatin. Cook and stir over medium heat until the mixture boils and thickens. Refrigerate for 30 minutes or until partially set (mixture should be the consistency of unbeaten egg white), stirring occasionally.

BEAT & FOLD Beat the egg whites in a medium bowl with an electric mixer until stiff but not dry. Beat the whipping cream in a medium bowl until soft peaks form. Gently fold the beaten egg whites and whipped cream into the thickened orange mixture using a wide rubber spatula. Spoon the mixture into a 1½ quart soufflé dish. Refrigerate for 6 hours or until set. Garnish with strips of orange peel, if desired.

Makes 6 servings
Per serving: 280 calories, 5g protein, 28g carbohydrates, 17g fat, 10g saturated fat, 157mg cholesterol, 50mg sodium

Root Beer Float Pops

Prep **10 MINUTES + FREEZING**

1½ cups cold water

1 cup vanilla ice cream

½ cup cold whole or 2% milk

½ cup sugar

2 teaspoons root beer concentrate

A classic soda-fountain drink turned into a blender-easy frozen treat. The key here is to use ice cold water and milk—it will take less time to freeze. For the tastiest results, use high-quality ice cream.

LET'S BEGIN Pour all the ingredients into an electric blender. Cover and blend until smooth.

POUR & FREEZE Pour mixture into ½-cup popsicle molds and place in freezer for 1½ hours, or until mixture is firm enough to support popsicle sticks. Insert popsicle sticks into each mold and freeze until completely set.

> *Makes 6 servings*
>
> *Per serving: 128 calories, 1g protein, 22g carbohydrates, 4g fat, 2g saturated fat, 13mg cholesterol, 32mg sodium*

Vanilla Custard Freeze

Prep **25 MINUTES**   *Cook* **4 MINUTES + FREEZING**

3 cups milk

1 cup cooked rice

¾ cup sugar

⅛ teaspoon salt

2 large eggs, beaten

2 cups cold whipping cream

1 tablespoon vanilla extract

All the flavor of the best homemade rice pudding, but served as a cold and refreshing ice cream. To speed up the cooling of the rice-custard mixture, set the pot in a large bowl of well-iced water. Place in the refrigerator, stirring every so often, until cold.

LET'S BEGIN Combine the milk, rice, sugar, salt, and eggs in a large saucepan. Cook over low heat, stirring constantly, for 4 to 6 minutes or until the mixture just begins to bubble. Remove from the heat. Add the cream and vanilla. Cool.

FREEZE & SERVE Prepare an electric ice cream freezer according to the manufacturer's directions. Pour the mixture into the freezer can and freeze as directed.

> *Makes 8 servings*
>
> *Per serving: 377 calories, 6g protein, 30g carbohydrates, 26g fat, 16g saturated fat, 144mg cholesterol, 191mg sodium*

CHOCOLATE MALLOW SWIRL PIE

Prep **20 MINUTES**   *Cook* **15 MINUTES + CHILLING**

4   cups miniature
     marshmallows

⅓   cup milk

¼   cup sugar

¼   cup unsweetened cocoa

3   tablespoons water

2   tablespoons butter or
     margarine

2   packages (8 ounces
     each) cream cheese,
     softened

2   teaspoons vanilla extract

1   cup (½ pint) cold
     whipping cream

1   package (9 ounces) extra
     serving-size graham
     cracker crumb crust

We love this pie with its graham cracker crust, but you can also use a chocolate-cookie crust for double chocolate satisfaction. Be sure to use miniature marshmallows because they melt extra quickly.

LET'S BEGIN Stir the marshmallows and milk in a medium saucepan. Cook over low heat, stirring constantly, until smooth. Refrigerate until the mixture thickens slightly.

BEAT & BLEND Stir the sugar, cocoa, water, and butter together in a small saucepan. Cook over low heat, stirring constantly, until the mixture boils. Refrigerate until cool. Beat the cream cheese and vanilla in a large bowl until fluffy. Stir the chilled marshmallow mixture until smooth, then beat into the cream cheese. Spoon 1½ cups into a medium bowl and set aside. Pour the cocoa mixture into the cheese mixture in the large bowl and stir to blend.

MIX & CHILL Beat whipping cream in a small bowl until stiff. Fold half the whipped cream into the vanilla filling. Fold the other half into the chocolate filling. Alternately spoon fillings into crust. Using a metal spatula or knife, swirl the filling for a marbled effect. Refrigerate about 6 hours or until set.

Makes 8 servings

Per serving: 638 calories, 7g protein, 55g carbohydrates, 42g fat, 23g saturated fat, 113mg cholesterol, 445mg sodium

CHEWY CHOCOLATE CHERRY SQUARES

Prep **20 MINUTES**   *Cook* **5 MINUTES + CHILLING**

18   chocolate sandwich cookies, crushed into crumbs

2   tablespoons butter or margarine, melted

1   cup boiling water

2   packages (4-serving size each) cherry flavor gelatin

⅔   cup maraschino cherries, drained, chopped

½   cup light corn syrup

2   cups thawed whipped topping

Chocolate and cherry make a classic flavor combination. Chocolate sandwich cookies make preparing the crust a snap and cherry flavor gelatin filled with lots of maraschino cherries makes it nice and fruity. Perfect for the after-school crowd.

LET'S BEGIN Mix 1 cup of the cookie crumbs with the melted butter in a medium bowl. Press mixture firmly onto the bottom of a 9-inch square baking pan. Reserve the remaining crumbs.

STIR & CHILL Stir the boiling water into the gelatin in a medium bowl for 2 minutes or until the gelatin is completely dissolved. Add the cherries and corn syrup and stir to blend. Refrigerate for 30 minutes or until slightly thickened. Pour the gelatin mixture over the crust. Refrigerate for 3 hours or until firm.

TOP & SERVE Spoon the whipped topping over the gelatin mixture. Just before serving, sprinkle the reserved cookie crumbs over the topping. Cut into squares. Cover and refrigerate any leftovers.

Makes 16 squares

Per square: 176 calories, 2g protein, 31g carbohydrates, 6g fat, 3g saturated fat, 4mg cholesterol, 155mg sodium

---

Cook to Cook

HOW DO YOU MELT CHOCOLATE WITHOUT IT LUMPING?

❝It's really easy . . . just keep water and steam away. That's what causes chocolate that you're melting to become grainy or lumpy. Pastry chefs call this problem "seizing."

To avoid disaster, **melt chocolate in a double boiler.** First, put about an inch of water in the bottom of the double boiler and bring the water to a simmer.

Remove the pan from the heat, place the top of the double boiler over the water, and drop the chocolate in. Then continue stirring until it's all melted and smooth.

A microwave is also great for melting chocolate smoothly. Put the chocolate in a thoroughly dry, microwave-safe bowl, then microwave on Medium for 1 min-

ute, and stir. Continue to microwave, stopping to stir every 15 to 30 seconds until the chocolate is smooth and melted.

Here's another tip: If you are **melting bars of chocolate, first chop them into small, even-sized pieces** so that they will melt quickly. Larger pieces take longer to melt and the chocolate may become too hot and burn.❞

MINI CHOCOLATE PIES

Prep **15 MINUTES**   *Cook* **10 MINUTES + CHILLING**

1   package (4-serving size) vanilla cook & serve pudding and pie filling mix

1   cup miniature semisweet chocolate chips

1   package (4 ounces) six single serve graham cracker pie crusts

Whipped topping

Additional miniature semisweet chocolate chips

Go for the gold—sprinkle fresh raspberries onto the whipped topping and top with long sprigs of fresh mint. The raspberries are the perfect flavor addition to the chocolate chip garnish.

LET'S BEGIN Prepare the pudding mix (not the instant one, please) as directed on the package. Immediately remove the pudding from the heat and stir in the chocolate chips. Stir until the chips melt, then let cool 5 minutes, stirring occasionally.

POUR & CHILL Place the pie crusts on a plate. Spoon the filling into the crusts. Press plastic wrap directly onto the surface of the pudding to prevent a skin from forming. Refrigerate for 3 hours or until firm. Garnish with whipped topping and miniature chocolate chips.

Makes 6 servings

Per serving: 338 calories, 2g protein, 49g carbohydrates, 17g fat, 7g saturated fat, 3mg cholesterol, 248mg sodium

SuperQuick
CLASSIC LEMON CURD

Prep **10 MINUTES**   *Cook* **5 MINUTES**

1   large egg

2   egg yolks

⅓   cup fresh lemon juice
         (juice of 2 lemons)

1½   teaspoons grated
         lemon peel

¾   cups sugar

¼   cup butter or margarine

Pinch of salt

Spread on hot toast, use to fill a layer cake, spoon into a jar for a holiday gift. It's so wonderful that folks keep finding more uses for it. It's yummy on warm scones and waffles too.

LET'S BEGIN In a medium saucepan, lightly beat the egg and yolks. Stir in the remaining ingredients.

STIR IT Cook over low heat, stirring constantly, until the mixture thickens, about 5 to 8 minutes. Serve warm or cold.

Makes 4 servings

Per serving: 300 calories, 3g protein, 38g carbohydrates, 16g fat, 7g saturated fat, 188mg cholesterol, 181mg sodium

SuperQuick
CHOCOLATE MOUSSE

Prep **10 MINUTES**

1⅓   cups cold whipping
         cream

½   cup sugar

⅓   cup unsweetened cocoa

1   teaspoon vanilla extract

¼   teaspoon imitation rum
         extract

Quick and delicious—it doesn't get better than this dessert gem. We love the combination of vanilla and rum; it adds flavor complexity without a lot of extra calories or work. Remember that the best way to whip cream is in a chilled bowl with chilled beaters, especially if the weather is warm.

LET'S BEGIN Beat together all the ingredients in a medium bowl until mixture is smooth and mounds softly.

FINAL TOUCH Spoon the mousse into a serving bowl, small ramekins, or dessert dishes. If desired, top each serving with a strawberry, a dollop of whipped cream, or chocolate curls.

Makes 4 servings

Per serving: 402 calories, 3g protein, 30g carbohydrates, 30g fat, 19g saturated fat, 109mg cholesterol, 32mg sodium

CRANBERRY & WHITE CHOCOLATE PARFAITS

Prep **15 MINUTES**   *Cook* **3 MINUTES + CHILLING**

1   can (16 ounces) whole berry cranberry sauce

1   tablespoon amaretto (almond flavor) liqueur, if desired

1   package (3.3 ounces) white chocolate or vanilla instant pudding and pie filling mix

1   cup milk

1   cup cold whipping cream

Additional whipped cream for garnish, if desired

The combination of cranberry and amaretto (almond-flavored liqueur) is elegant and delicious. But you can use other liqueurs, including Grand Marnier (orange-flavored), Nocello (walnut-flavored), or Framboise (raspberry-flavored).

LET'S BEGIN Stir the cranberry sauce and amaretto in a small bowl. Set aside. Combine the pudding mix and milk in the small bowl of an electric mixer. Beat on low speed for 30 seconds. Add whipping cream and beat on medium speed for 2 to 3 minutes or until soft peaks form.

LAYER IT Spoon alternate layers of the pudding and cranberry sauce into parfait glasses or stemmed wine glasses. Refrigerate at least 30 minutes or until set. Garnish with additional whipped cream, if desired.

Makes 6 servings

Per serving: 342 calories, 2g protein, 48g carbohydrates, 16g fat, 10g saturated fat, 58mg cholesterol, 263mg sodium

FLORIDA KEY LIME PIE

Prep **10 MINUTES** *Chill* **2 HOURS**

1   can (14 ounces) sweetened condensed milk

½   cup fresh lime juice

1   teaspoon grated lime zest

1   package (6 ounces) prepared graham cracker pie crust

2   cups frozen whipped topping, thawed

8   thin lime slices (optional)

Key lime pie is one of those no-bake desserts that has stood the test of time. In the sunny state of Florida, they make this pie only with the small authentic key limes. If you can't find them, look for a bottle of key lime juice or use the regular limes from your supermarket. To get the most juice out of the limes, first roll them on the counter using a little pressure. Tip: Grate the lime zest before you juice them.

LET'S BEGIN Combine the sweetened condensed milk and the lime juice in medium bowl and beat with an electric mixer until well combined. Stir in the lime zest.

FILL & CHILL Pour the milk mixture into the crust and top with the whipped topping. Refrigerate for 2 hours or until set. Garnish with the lime slices, if you wish.

Makes 8 servings

Per serving: 385 calories, 3g protein, 34g carbohydrates, 13g fat, 7g saturated fat, 7mg cholesterol, 167mg sodium

STRAWBERRY-LEMON PARFAIT

Prep **25 MINUTES + CHILLING**

½ cup cold whipping cream

½ cup prepared lemon curd, usually sold in jars

Grated peel of 1 lemon

2 pints fresh strawberries, stemmed and sliced

Fresh mint leaves or twisted lemon slices, for garnish

We have the English to thank for wonderful lemon curd. They cook a mixture of lemon juice, sugar, butter, and egg yolks until it's thick and creamy. It's delicious on warm scones or biscuits and perfect in these berry parfaits. You can purchase lemon curd ready made; it can be found in the jam and jelly or gourmet section of your supermarket.

LET'S BEGIN Using a medium bowl whip the cream to form stiff peaks. In another medium bowl fold ¼ cup of the whipped cream into the lemon curd. Blend thoroughly, then fold in the remaining cream and lemon peel. Chill for 30 minutes.

LAYER IT To serve, spoon 3 layers of the strawberries and 2 layers of lemon cream in each of 4 stemmed glasses, beginning and ending with the strawberries. Garnish with mint or thin lemon slices. Serve with small crisp cookies.

Makes 4 servings

Per serving: 215 calories, 2g protein, 26g carbohydrates, 12g fat, 7g saturated fat, 43mg cholesterol, 36mg sodium

---

Food Facts

THE HISTORY OF KEY LIME PIE

Enjoying a wedge of this creamy, sweet-tart pie is like taking a trip to Florida. It seems that Key West cooks have been dishing up this special dessert since the 1890s, soon after Gale Borden began canning sweetened condensed milk. Until that time, due to the lack of refrigeration, fresh milk did not keep well.

Home bakers in the Florida Keys are rather finicky about their pies: they use only the native, tiny Florida Key limes—not regular Persian limes. They also always use sweetened condensed milk and never, never tint the filling green!

In the early 1900s, Key Lime Pie was always made with a flaky pastry. But nowadays, a graham cracker crust is preferred by most cooks.

To top it all off, a fluffy meringue was most often the crowning glory in the early days, but now Key Lime Pies are topped with lots of creamy whipped cream. Often cooks garnish it with fine shavings of lime zest.

STRAWBERRY TIRAMISU

Prep **25 MINUTES + CHILLING**

2   packages (8 ounces each) Neufchatel cheese, softened

¾   cup confectioners' sugar

1   container (8 ounces) frozen light whipped topping, thawed

1   cup strong coffee, at room temperature

3   tablespoons coffee-flavored liqueur (optional)

24   ladyfingers split in half

2   teaspoons unsweetened cocoa

1½   pints strawberries (18 ounces total), stemmed and sliced

Sometimes referred to as an "Italian Trifle," this ethereal dessert mingles the flavors of cheese, coffee, and cocoa in heavenly light layers.

LET'S BEGIN In a large mixer bowl, beat the cheese and sugar until well blended. Using a rubber spatula, gently fold in the whipped topping. In another small bowl, combine the coffee and liqueur, if desired. Line an 8-inch square glass dish with enough ladyfinger halves, rounded-sides-down, to cover the bottom. You may need to cut the ladyfingers to fit the dish.

LAYER IT Spoon ⅓ cup of the coffee mixture evenly over the ladyfingers. Spread about 1 cup of the cheese mixture evenly over the ladyfingers. Next, layer 1 rounded cup of the sliced strawberries over the cheese. Repeat the layers two more times, ending with the cheese. Cover the tiramisu and the remaining strawberries and refrigerate for 1 hour or up to 24 hours.

SIFT & SERVE To serve, sift the cocoa over the cheese. Arrange the reserved strawberry slices over the top. Serve immediately.

Makes 12 servings

Per serving: 250 calories, 7g protein, 28g carbohydrates, 13g fat, 8g saturated fat, 105mg cholesterol, 200mg sodium

FRUITY MOCHA MOUSSE

Prep **15 MINUTES + CHILLING**

¾   cup semisweet chocolate
     morsels

2   cups cold whipping
     cream

2   tablespoons
     confectioners' sugar

1   can (16 ounces) jellied
     cranberry sauce

¼   cup light corn syrup

¼   cup coffee flavored
     liqueur

You can also make this cranberry and chocolate treat in a pretty cut-glass bowl for a holiday dinner or buffet. Garnish it with a border of whipped cream and top with sugared fresh cranberries and little sprigs of fresh mint. So festive!

LET'S BEGIN Place ½ cup of the chocolate morsels in a medium, microwavable bowl. Microwave on High (100%) for 2 minutes or until the morsels melt. Using an electric mixer on high speed, add ½ cup of the cream to the chocolate, 2 tablespoons at a time, mixing well after each addition. Gradually add remaining cream and confectioners' sugar, whipping until stiff peaks form. Spoon into individual dessert dishes. Chill at least 1 hour before serving.

COOK & COOL Combine the remaining ingredients in a medium saucepan and stir over medium heat until smooth, whisking frequently. Cool to room temperature. Spoon the cranberry mixture over the mousse.

Makes 8 servings

Per serving: 586 calories, 3g protein, 61g carbohydrates, 36g fat, 22g saturated fat, 110mg cholesterol, 61mg sodium

Easy Pumpkin Ice Cream, page 107

Ice Cream Creations

If you've ever been lucky enough to lick the paddle after hand-churning a batch of homemade ice cream, you know what a real treat it is. And even if you don't have an ice cream freezer, you can bring back those memories. Whirl up some ice cream in a blender, process a can of frozen peaches into a delectable sorbet, or turn a can of cranberry sauce into a classic Italian granita. But don't stop there! Enjoy our quick-as-a-wink creations of ice cream sandwiches and banana splits, and our simple way to whip up an ice cream pie—all with little fuss but lots of smiles from friends and family. Enjoy our new frozen dessert creations, without turning a crank!

SuperQuick
BERRY BLENDER ICE CREAM

Prep **10 MINUTES**

1   package (10 ounces) frozen sliced strawberries in syrup

¼   cup whipping cream

¼   cup egg substitute

1   teaspoon lemon juice

Here's homemade ice cream in just 10 minutes—with no freezing or chilling! The secret is the frozen strawberries.

LET'S BEGIN Dip the package of frozen strawberries into hot water for 20 seconds. Remove the strawberries and cut into chunks the size of ice cubes.

BLEND & SERVE Combine the cream and egg substitute in a blender or food processor. Cover and blend for 2 seconds. Drop in the frozen strawberries, a chunk at a time. Cover and blend until smooth, turning on and off and scraping the sides of the container as needed. Blend in the lemon juice. Immediately spoon the ice cream into serving dishes.

NOTE: Ice cream can be made ahead, covered, and stored in the freezer. Remove 15 minutes before serving.

Makes 2 servings

Per serving: 267 calories, 5g protein, 38g carbohydrates, 12g fat, 7g saturated fat, 41mg cholesterol, 71mg sodium

---

Cook to Cook

WHAT ARE THE BEST ICE CREAM MAKERS?

"*The most basic ice cream maker is a hand- or electric-crank model* that consists of a bucket with a smaller canister that fits inside along with a dasher (often called a paddle or stirrer). The space between the bucket and canister is filled with rock salt and ice and the canister contains the ice cream mixture. As you turn the crank, the ice freezes the cream, finally turning the mixture into delicious ice cream.

There is also a very popular model that has a *coolant-filled metal canister that you chill in the freezer.* No ice or salt is required. The ice cream mixture is poured into the canister, which is placed inside a plastic container. It comes in a hand-crank or electric model.

The Rolls Royce of ice cream makers is a canister that sits inside a fancy housing that you can place on your counter. Once the canister is filled, you flip a switch and the machine automatically chills and churns the ice cream mixture. That's the easiest way to get homemade ice cream!"

SIMPLE PEACH SORBET

Prep **5 MINUTES + FREEZING**

2   cans (15 ounces each) light yellow cling sliced peaches

1   teaspoon vanilla extract

Fresh mint leaves (optional)

Pick up a couple of cans of peaches and turn them into sorbet! Pop them in the freezer one day, then whirl them up in the food processor the next. Nothing could be simpler, or more delicious!

LET'S BEGIN Place one unopened can of peaches in the freezer until solid (about 24 hours). Submerge the unopened frozen can in very hot tap water for 1 minute. Open and pour any thawed syrup into a food processor bowl. Remove the peaches from the can and carefully cut into 8 chunks. Place the peaches and vanilla in a food processor (blender or mini-processors not recommended). Process until smooth, scraping the blade as needed.

SERVE IT UP Serve immediately or store in the freezer. Garnish with the remaining can of peach slices and fresh mint, if desired.

Makes 4 servings

Per serving: 106 calories, 0g protein, 26g carbohydrates, 0g fat, 0g saturated fat, 0mg cholesterol, 17mg sodium

Food Facts

THE FIRST ICE CREAM CONE

It's hard to imagine a time when ice cream cones didn't exist. But this ideal ice cream holder didn't make an appearance until the 1904 St. Louis World's Fair.

As with many new ideas, it happened pretty much by chance.

As the story goes, an ice cream vendor at the fair was right next to a fellow who sold round waffles. A clever customer bought a waffle, placed his scoop of ice cream on top, and ate it like an open-faced sandwich. Unfortunately, his com-panion did the same thing, but his ice cream slid right off. The observant waffle maker, after some thought, rolled a hot waffle into a cone shape, and asked the ice cream vendor to fill it. And a tradition was born.

SuperQuick
TROPI-NANA SPLIT

Prep **10 MINUTES**

3	bananas
1	pint vanilla ice cream
1	pint chocolate ice cream
1	pint raspberry or strawberry ice cream
1	jar (24 ounces) refrigerated tropical mixed fruit, drained
¾	cup cold whipping cream, whipped
⅓	cup toasted coconut
⅓	cup chopped nuts, toasted

Fresh bing cherries or maraschino cherries

The banana split just took a holiday in the tropical isles. All those ingredients of the "split" are here, stacked up in individual servings.

LET'S BEGIN Halve the bananas lengthwise and then cut in half crosswise.

LET'S EAT Arrange 2 banana slices in each of 6 serving bowls. Top each serving with scoops of vanilla, chocolate, and raspberry ice cream. Spoon the fruit over the ice cream and top with about 2 tablespoons whipped cream, 1 tablespoon coconut, and 1 tablespoon chopped nuts. Top with a cherry.

Makes 6 servings

Per serving: 592 calories, 7g protein, 75g carbohydrates, 31g fat, 18g saturated fat, 88mg cholesterol, 138mg sodium

TROPICAL PINK SORBET

Prep **10 MINUTES + FREEZING**

1	can (15½ ounces) chilled, tropical fruit salad, drained
¾	cup (6 ounces) pink grapefruit juice blend

Many sorbets are made light, fruity, and refreshing. This one's no exception! And it freezes right inside the freezer.

LET'S BEGIN Combine both ingredients in the container of a food processor. Process until the mixture is smooth, about 20 seconds. Pour mixture into a heavy plastic container. Freeze just until firm, about 2 hours.

POUR & FREEZE Break the frozen mixture into pieces and return to the food processor. Process just until smooth, about 30 seconds. Return the mixture to the plastic container and freeze until firm, about 3 hours. Remove from freezer about 10 minutes before serving. Spoon into serving dishes.

Makes 6 servings

Per serving: 56 calories, 0g protein, 14g carbohydrates, 0g fat, 0g saturated fat, 0mg cholesterol, 5mg sodium

BANANA SPLITS

Prep **35 MINUTES + FREEZING**   *Cook* **30 MINUTES + COOLING**

CRUST

3	cups graham cracker crumbs
2/3	cup butter or margarine, melted
6	tablespoons sugar

FILLING

3	large bananas
1	carton (1/2 gallon) Neapolitan ice cream
1	cup chopped walnuts
1	package (6 ounces) semisweet chocolate chips
1/2	cup butter or margarine
2	cups sifted confectioners' sugar
1	can (12 ounces) evaporated milk
1	teaspoon vanilla extract
2	cups (1 pint) cold whipping cream

The soda jerk at the corner drugstore was a genius. He knew just how to make those delicious creations called banana splits. We've taken all those flavors and layered them into an ice loaf that's ideal for a party.

LET'S BEGIN Blend the graham cracker crumbs, melted butter, and 6 tablespoons sugar in a medium bowl. Remove 1/2 cup and set aside. Press the remaining crumb mixture over the bottom of a 15 × 10 × 1-inch jelly-roll pan to form the crust.

LAYER IT Cut the bananas crosswise into 1/2-inch slices and arrange in a layer over the crust. Slice the ice cream into 9 slices and arrange on top of the banana slices. Sprinkle the chopped walnuts over the top. Freeze until the ice cream is firm, about 30 minutes. Combine chocolate pieces and 1/2 cup butter in a heavy, medium saucepan. Cook and stir over low heat until the chocolate and butter melt. Stir in the confectioners' sugar and evaporated milk and stir constantly until mixture is thick and smooth. Remove from the heat and stir in vanilla. Let stand at room temperature until cool, about 20 minutes. Pour the cooled chocolate mixture over the frozen mixture and freeze until the chocolate layer is firm, about 30 minutes.

BEAT & FREEZE Beat the cream in a medium bowl with an electric mixer until stiff peaks form. Spread evenly over the chocolate layer. Sprinkle with the reserved crumbs. Cover and freeze until firm, about 1 hour. Before serving, let stand at room temperature about 5 minutes. Cut into 24 squares.

Makes 24 squares

Per square: 450 calories, 6g protein, 42g carbohydrates, 30g fat, 15g saturated fat, 73mg cholesterol, 167mg sodium

CHOCOLATE LOVER'S ICE CREAM PIE

Prep **20 MINUTES + FREEZING**

24   crisp chocolate chip cookies, crushed (2 cups crumbs)

⅓   cup butter or margarine, melted

1   quart of your favorite chocolate ice cream, slightly softened

2   cups chocolate-flavored syrup, if desired

1   cup whipping cream, sweetened, whipped, if desired

Chocolate chip cookies, broken into pieces, if desired

Chocolate appears, and reappears, three different ways in this spectacular frozen pie—in the chocolate chip cookie crust, in the chocolate ice cream filling, and again in the drizzle of chocolate syrup on top. Make it for any chocolate lover you know as a birthday surprise. Just add candles!

LET'S BEGIN Stir together the crushed cookies and butter in a medium bowl. Press the crumb mixture on the bottom and up the side of a 9-inch pie pan. Freeze for 10 minutes or until firm.

SPREAD & FREEZE Spread the ice cream over the crust. Cover and freeze for 6 hours or until firm.

FINAL TOUCH Just before serving, drizzle the pie with the chocolate syrup. Top with the sweetened whipped cream and chocolate chip cookie pieces, if desired.

Makes 8 servings

Per serving: 340 calories, 4g protein, 36g carbohydrates, 21g fat, 11g saturated fat, 60mg cholesterol, 250mg sodium

Food Facts

HOW DO YOU CUT FROZEN DESSERTS?

Always use a sturdy, sharp knife to cut frozen ice cream, cakes, or pies. A chef's knife is perfect.

Hold the knife under hot water before making that first slice. Then dip it into hot water after making each slice.

When cutting a cake or pie, first insert the tip of the knife into the center of the dessert. Then with a sawing motion cut through to the edge.

When scooping ice cream out of a container, warm it in the microwave on High for about 30 seconds to make it easier to scoop.

Dip your ice cream scoop into hot water between "scoops."

CITRUS YOGURT SUNDAES
Prep **15 MINUTES**

1   cup (8 ounces) low-fat vanilla yogurt

1   teaspoon freshly grated orange peel

1   teaspoon freshly grated grapefruit peel

2   grapefruit, peeled and sectioned

2   oranges, peeled and cut into half-cartwheel slices

2   bananas, sliced

1   cup blueberries, strawberries, raspberries, or seedless grapes

1   teaspoon sugar

¼   teaspoon cinnamon

Sprightly grapefruit peel adds a unique twist to this fruit cup. It's fresh, filled with a colorful combination of fresh fruits, and weighs in at only 140 calories per serving.

LET'S BEGIN In a medium bowl, combine the yogurt and orange and grapefruit peel. Cover and chill for 30 minutes.

MIX & CHILL In a large bowl, combine all the remaining ingredients. Cover and chill for 30 minutes. To serve, spoon the fruit into individual dessert dishes. Top with the yogurt.

Makes 6 servings

Per serving: 140 calories, 4g protein, 32g carbohydrates, 1g fat, 0g saturated fat, 2mg cholesterol, 26mg sodium

---

Cooking Basics

HINTS ON MAKING HEAVENLY ICE CREAMS

Here are some things we like to keep in mind when making homemade ice creams, sorbet, and sherbets:

• Though we like our ice cream sweet, never add extra sugar to a recipe. Too much sugar will prevent the ice cream from freezing properly, and it will be too soft.

• Too little sugar means your ice cream or ice will be too hard.

• When making French ice cream (the kind that starts with a cooked custard), never allow the custard to boil. The mixture will curdle and your ice cream will be grainy.

• For custard ice creams, cool the custard first, then add the flavorings right before you start freezing the mixture. Many flavorings used in ice creams are volatile. If added to the hot custard as it cooks, much of the flavor will cook away.

• When freezing ice creams or ices in your freezer, be sure to stir by hand several times to prevent ice crystals from forming.

ALMOND MOCHA ICE CREAM

Prep **15 MINUTES**   *Microwave* **3 MINUTES + FREEZING**

4   ounces semisweet
    chocolate

1   can (14 ounces)
    sweetened condensed
    milk (not evaporated
    milk)

3   tablespoons instant
    coffee powder or 1½
    tablespoons freeze-dried
    instant coffee

½   cup water

2   cups cold whipping
    cream

1   cup chopped almonds,
    toasted

It wasn't so long ago that everyone gathered on the village green for an old-fashioned summer picnic. The highlight was always the hand-cranked ice cream at the end of the day. There never seemed to be enough. This recipe revisits those times, for it's just as rich and creamy as the ice cream at those village gatherings. But the best part is that this one can freeze on its own—without any hand-churning from you.

LET'S BEGIN Place the chocolate in a large microwavable bowl. Microwave on Medium (50%) for 3 minutes or until the chocolate is smooth and shiny. Stir once after each minute.

Add the condensed milk, coffee powder, and water and stir to blend. Use a wire whisk, if necessary to remove lumps. Chill, stirring occasionally, for 1 hour or until the mixture is cold.

FOLD & FREEZE Whip the cream with an electric mixer in a medium bowl until stiff. Fold the cream and almonds into the chilled chocolate mixture with a rubber spatula until no streaks remain. Turn the mixture into metal loaf pans and freeze for 3 to 4 hours or until firm. To serve, scoop ice cream into serving dishes and garnish with whole, blanched almonds and chocolate curls, if desired.

Makes about 1½ quarts, about 12 servings (½ cup each)

Per serving: 361 calories, 7g protein, 28g carbohydrates, 27g fat, 13g saturated fat, 66mg cholesterol, 59mg sodium

On the Menu

Turn a birthday party into a
happening by creating a
sundae party. Set out sundae
dishes and spoons (and plenty
of festive napkins!) and have
a ball! Place the sundae
fixings in festive bowls—
and don't forget spoons.

Various ice creams

Sweetened whipped cream

Sauce (caramel,
butterscotch, chocolate,
strawberry, blueberry)

Sliced strawberries,
raspberries, blueberries

Marshmallow fluff

Chopped nuts (walnuts,
peanuts, pecans)

Sprinkles (chocolate and
rainbow)

Maraschino cherries

Various candy bits

SuperQuick
ICE CREAMWICHES
Prep **5 MINUTES**

Here's the perfect treat for little hands to make—ice cream sandwiches made from waffles. They're those round ones that come frozen and ready to eat. No cooking here—just lots of good eating.

2   **round prepared waffles**

1   **tablespoon strawberry fruit spread**

1   **scoop vanilla ice cream**

LET'S BEGIN Toast two round prepared waffles (found in freezer section of supermarket). Spread one waffle with strawberry fruit spread and one scoop of vanilla ice cream. Place the other waffle on top and enjoy! Repeat for multiple servings.

Makes 1 serving
Per serving: 358 calories, 7g protein, 55g carbohydrates, 13g fat, 6g saturated fat, 32mg cholesterol, 603mg sodium

BLUSHING SNOWBALLS

Prep **15 MINUTES**   *Freeze* **5 HOURS**

2   tablespoons powdered strawberry-flavored milk beverage mix

1   teaspoon water

1⅓ cups flaked coconut

6   large scoops vanilla ice cream

½   cup chocolate-flavored syrup

Bring back memories of a childhood treat with coconut-coated ice cream served under a drizzle of rich chocolate syrup. Make the ice cream balls and freeze them on a waxed paper-lined baking sheet for a few minutes to harden before rolling in the coconut.

LET'S BEGIN Combine the beverage mix and the water in small bowl and stir until well combined. Stir in the coconut until well coated.

ROLL & FREEZE Scoop the ice cream into balls and roll in the coconut mixture. Freeze for 5 hours or until firm.

DRIZZLE & SERVE To serve, place each snowball in a serving dish and drizzle with the syrup.

Makes 6 servings

Per serving: 425 calories, 5g protein, 58g carbohydrates, 20g fat, 14g saturated fat, 58mg cholesterol, 180mg sodium

EASY PUMPKIN ICE CREAM

Prep **5 MINUTES**   *Freeze* **5 HOURS**

2   quarts vanilla ice cream, softened

1   can (30 ounces) pumpkin pie mix

Why not forget about the pie at this year's Thanksgiving feast and serve this super-easy ice cream instead? Dress it up with a drizzle of caramel sauce and a sprinkle of chopped walnuts.

FIX IT FAST Combine the ice cream and pumpkin pie mix in a large bowl and stir until well mixed. Freeze in an ice cream maker according to manufacturer's directions.

NOTE: To make the ice cream without using an ice cream maker, cover the mixture and freeze for 2 hours. Beat the ice cream with an electric mixer for 30 seconds and then freeze for 3 more hours or until firm.

Makes 16 servings

Per serving: 188 calories, 3g protein, 28g carbohydrates, 8g fat, 4g saturated fat, 29mg cholesterol, 123mg sodium

Time Savers

FAST ICE CREAM BLENDS

"Blends" have really caught many people's attention lately. It's truly a chance to have ice cream your way!

The method for making blends is really quite simple! All it takes is a container of ice cream, such as vanilla, chocolate, coffee, or strawberry. Then add the key ingredient: lots of imagination to stir, mix, and conjure up some of the most fantastic ice cream combos in the world!

DOUBLE YOUR PLEASURE Slightly soften two favorite flavors of ice cream, sorbet, or one of each: think raspberry sorbet and vanilla cream, chocolate and coffee ice cream, rocky road and strawberry ice cream. Spoon them into a bowl and gently stir to slightly blend and swirl the colors. Then quickly put the blend into a bowl, cover tightly, and freeze until nice and firm.

CRUNCH, CRUNCH! Peek into your pantry to see what tantalizing extras the shelves hold that will take a simple ice cream flavor to new heights: granola, Rice Krispies, toasted slivered almonds, chocolate chips, hot fudge or caramel sauce, lemon curd, crushed gingersnap cookies, chopped chocolate, fresh berries, shredded coconut (toasted or not) can all be folded into slightly softened ice cream. Go wild . . . you can't go wrong.

CRANBERRY ORANGE GRANITA

Prep **5 MINUTES + FREEZING**

1   can (16 ounces) jellied cranberry sauce

1   split or small bottle (187 ml) champagne or ¾ cup ginger ale

2   tablespoons orange juice

Mint leaves, for garnish

When you start this frozen Italian ice from champagne, it's bound to be a big hit. Add the heavenly flavor of cranberries and you have a winner. Why not plan it for your next party?

LET'S BEGIN Combine all the ingredients except the mint leaves in the container of a food processor. Process until the mixture is smooth. Pour into a non-metal 8-inch square pan. Freeze just until firm, about 3 hours.

POUR & FREEZE Break up into pieces and process again until smooth. Return cranberry mixture to pan and freeze for 2 hours or until firm. Remove from the freezer 5 minutes before serving to make scooping easier. Garnish with mint leaves.

Makes 4 servings

Per serving: 198 calories, 0g protein, 44g carbohydrates, 0g fat, 0g saturated fat, 0mg cholesterol, 24mg sodium

CHERRY SPUMONI

Prep **20 MINUTES + CHILLING & FREEZING**

2   cups cold whipping cream

⅔   cup (7 ounces) sweetened condensed milk (not evaporated milk)

½   teaspoon rum-flavored extract

1   can (21 ounces) cherry pie filling

½   cup slivered almonds, chopped

½   cup miniature chocolate morsels

This classic molded ice cream treat comes from Italy. Traditionally, it starts with two different flavors of ice cream, often chocolate and vanilla. It's then layered into an ice cream mold between sweetened whipped cream, spiked with rum, and mixed with colorful candied fruits and nuts. Our recipe skips the ice cream and uses cherry pie filling and chocolate chips to flavor the whipped cream.

LET'S BEGIN Combine the cream, sweetened condensed milk, and rum extract in a large bowl. Refrigerate for 30 minutes. Beat the chilled cream mixture until soft peaks form. Be careful not to overbeat. Gently fold in the remaining ingredients. Pour into an 8-inch square pan.

FREEZE & SERVE Cover and freeze about 4 hours or until firm. Allow the spumoni to stand about 5 minutes before serving. Scoop out to serve.

Makes 8 servings

Per serving: 475 calories, 6g protein, 45g carbohydrates, 32g fat, 17g saturated fat, 91g cholesterol, 69mg sodium

Very Berry French Toast, page 134

Weekend Desserts

Go ahead and splurge—it's the weekend! Whip up one of those decadent, delicious cheesecakes your family loves. It's here, but even easier than you ever thought possible, for our cakes don't need an oven. But that's not all. You'll find rich rice puddings, batches of fudge, and even brownies that mix up easily, without baking. And for that weekend dinner when friends come to call, we've included those fancy dessert crepes laced with orange liqueur that everyone loves—plus a couple of deep, rich chocolate fondues just made for dunking. And to impress your guests even more, we've added a fancy way to decorate dessert plates. Why not? It's a party!

EASY & ELEGANT CHEESECAKE

Prep **20 MINUTES** *Cook* **2 MINUTES** *Chill* **3 HOURS**

CRUST

1¼ cups graham cracker crumbs

⅓ cup butter or margarine, melted

2 teaspoons sugar

CHEESECAKE

1 package (12 ounces) semisweet chocolate morsels

1 envelope (.25 ounces) unflavored gelatin

⅔ cup water

2 packages (8 ounces) cream cheese, softened

1 can (14 ounces) sweetened condensed milk

1 cup heavy whipping cream, whipped

We love gelatin-based cheesecakes, because you can count on them to be light and delicate—and you don't have to turn on your oven! Serve it elegantly by piping or spooning a ring of whipped cream around the edge. Then blanket the cream with casual chocolate curls made by drawing a vegetable peeler across a bar of chocolate.

LET'S BEGIN To make the crust, combine the graham cracker crumbs, butter, and sugar in a medium bowl and stir until well mixed. Press the mixture into the bottom of a 9-inch springform pan.

MELT & STIR Place the morsels in a medium microwave-safe bowl. Microwave on High for 1 minute and stir until the morsels are melted and smooth. If necessary, microwave for an additional 30 seconds at a time, just until smooth when stirred. Let the chocolate cool. Sprinkle the gelatin over the water in a small saucepan and let it stand for 1 minute. Warm the mixture over low heat, stirring constantly, just until gelatin dissolves. Remove from the heat.

FILL & CHILL Combine the cream cheese and the cooled chocolate in a large bowl and beat with an electric mixer until fluffy. Gradually beat in the sweetened condensed milk. Stir in the gelatin mixture and then fold in the whipped cream. Pour into the prepared crust. Refrigerate for 3 hours or until set. Run a knife around the edge of the cheesecake before removing the side of the springform pan.

Makes 16 servings

Per serving: 350 calories, 5g protein, 22g carbohydrates, 27g fat, 16g saturated fat, 63mg cholesterol, 155mg sodium

CHEESECAKE PIES

To make two pies, press crumb mixture into two 9-inch pie plates. Or two prepared (9 ounces each) graham cracker crusts can be substituted for the 9-inch springform crust. Divide the filling evenly between the two crusts and refrigerate as directed above.

BLACK-BOTTOM MINI CHEESECAKES

Prep **20 MINUTES** *Microwave* **2 MINUTES + CHILLING**

6	tablespoons butter or margarine
1	package (11.1 ounces) no-bake cheesecake crust mix
2	tablespoons sugar
3	squares (3 ounces) semi-sweet baking chocolate
1½	cups cold milk
3	cups mixed fresh fruit (raspberries, blueberries, sliced peeled kiwifruit)
¼	cup apricot preserves, melted

Black bottom usually refers to a classic American pie that has a rich chocolate-custard layer on the bottom and a rum-flavored custard layer on top. Here, a thin layer of drizzled chocolate is the black bottom, while an easy no-bake cheesecake mix is the luscious filling. After rinsing the berries for the topping, be sure to pat them thoroughly dry.

LET'S BEGIN Melt 5 tablespoons of the butter in a medium microwavable bowl. Add the packet of crust mix and sugar and stir to blend. Spoon 2 teaspoons of the crust evenly into each of 36 paper-lined miniature muffin pan cups. Press firmly onto bottoms of cups. Mix the remaining 1 tablespoon of butter and the chocolate in a small microwavable bowl. Microwave on High for 1 minute or until butter and chocolate are completely melted when stirred. Drizzle the chocolate evenly over crusts.

MIX & CHILL Combine the milk and packet of filling mix in a medium bowl. Beat with an electric mixer on low speed just until filling is moistened, then beat on medium speed 3 minutes. (Filling will be thick.) Spoon filling evenly into prepared cups. Refrigerate for 1 hour or until set.

TOP & SERVE Arrange fruit on top of the cheesecakes, then brush with preserves. Cover and refrigerate until ready to serve. Store leftover cheesecakes in refrigerator.

Makes 12 servings, 3 cheesecakes each

Per serving: 260 calories, 3g protein, 38g carbohydrates, 11g fat, 4g saturated fat, 5mg cholesterol, 270mg sodium

TROPICAL CHEESECAKE

Prep **25 MINUTES + CHILLING**

1   package (8 ounces) cream cheese, softened

⅓   cup sugar

1   tub (8 ounces) whipped topping, thawed

2   kiwifruit, peeled, quartered, sliced

1   medium mango, peeled, chopped

1   cup coconut, toasted

1   graham cracker piecrust (6 ounces)

One bite of this ethereal dessert and you'll think you're on an exotic tropical island in the South Pacific. The coconut can be toasted in a large toaster oven, if you prefer. Just be sure to keep an eye on it because it can quickly burn.

LET'S BEGIN Beat the cream cheese and sugar in a large bowl with a wire whisk or electric mixer until well blended.

FIX IT UP Add whipped topping; stir gently until well blended. Reserve ¼ cup each kiwi, mango, and coconut for garnish. Stir remaining kiwi, mango, and coconut into cream cheese mixture. Spoon into crust.

EAT IT UP Refrigerate 3 hours or until set. Top with reserved mango, kiwi, and coconut. Store leftover cheesecake in refrigerator.

Makes 8 servings

Per serving: 420 calories, 3g protein, 43g carbohydrates, 26g fat, 17g saturated fat, 30mg cholesterol, 260mg sodium

CHERRY CHEESE HEART

Prep **20 MINUTES**   *Chill* **4 HOURS**

3   envelopes (.25 ounce) unflavored gelatin

½   cup sugar

2   cups milk

2   cans (21 ounces each) cherry pie filling

2   packages (8 ounces each) cream cheese, softened

¼   cup almond flavored liqueur

3   cups frozen whipped topping, thawed, divided

⅓   cup sliced almonds, for garnish

When it's Valentine's Day, and even if it's not, here's the perfect dessert to fix for that special someone. Canned cherry pie filling colors the creamy cheese red for the occasion, and a little liqueur adds that touch of elegance. Decorate with more cherries and cream, light some candles, put on some romantic music, and you're all set!

LET'S BEGIN Mix the gelatin and sugar in a small saucepan. Stir in 1½ cups of the milk. Stir over medium heat until the gelatin dissolves completely. Remove from the heat. Drain 1 can of the pie filling, reserving the syrup. Cover and refrigerate the cherries for garnish.

POUR & CHILL In a food processor or electric blender, process the reserved cherry syrup and remaining 1 can pie filling and blend until smooth. Pour into a large bowl and beat in the remaining ½ cup milk, liqueur, and gelatin mixture with a wire whisk. Refrigerate for 30 minutes or until mixture is slightly thickened. Fold 2 cups of the whipped topping into the cherry mixture. Pour into a lightly oiled 2-quart cup mold. Chill for 4 hours or until firm.

FINAL TOUCH Run the tip of a small knife around the top of the mold, then dip the mold into warm water for 10 seconds to loosen. Place a large plate over the mold and carefully invert to unmold. Garnish with the remaining 1 cup whipped topping, drained cherries, and almonds.

Makes 10 servings

Per serving: 470 calories, 8g protein, 54g carbohydrates, 23g fat, 15g saturated fat, 55mg cholesterol, 181mg sodium

PEPPERMINT CLOUD RICE PIE

Prep **5 MINUTES**   *Cook* **23 MINUTES + CHILLING**

How clever is this pie! A decadently creamy rice pudding mixture that is spooned into a store-bought chocolate crumb crust and topped with peppermint candy-infused whipped cream. Sprinkle the extra peppermint bits on top just before serving so they don't melt.

3	cups cooked rice
3	cups milk
½	cup sugar
½	teaspoon salt
2	large eggs
2	tablespoons butter or margarine
1	teaspoon vanilla extract
1	packaged chocolate cookie crumb crust, 9 inches
⅓	cup crushed peppermint candy
1	container (8 ounces) frozen whipped topping, thawed

LET'S BEGIN Combine the rice, 2½ cups milk, sugar, and salt in a medium saucepan. Bring to a boil over medium-high heat, then reduce the heat to medium-low and simmer for 20 to 25 minutes, or until very thick and creamy, stirring occasionally.

COOK & COOL Beat the eggs with the remaining ½ cup milk in a small bowl, then stir into the rice mixture. Cook for 2 minutes over low heat. Remove from the heat and add the butter and vanilla. Cool. Spread the mixture into the crumb crust. Refrigerate for at least 2 hours.

TOP & SERVE Fold the crushed candy into the whipped topping. Swirl onto the top of the pie. Garnish with bits of peppermint candy, if desired.

Makes 8 servings

Per serving: 490 calories, 8g protein, 65g carbohydrates, 21g fat, 11g saturated fat, 71mg cholesterol, 682mg sodium

---

On the Menu

Fast and fabulous delicious desserts can come from various sources, many in an instant, on your way home.

FROM THE FARMER'S MARKET
Fresh Peaches and Blueberries on Shortcakes or Angel Cake

FROM THE LOCAL BAKERY
Fresh Fruit Pie with Crème Fraiche

FROM THE GRILL
Caramelized Bananas

FROM YOUR FREEZER
Layered Ice Cream Parfaits

FROM THE MICROWAVE
Blushing Poached Pears

CHERRY-CINNAMON CRÈME ANGLAISE

Prep **10 MINUTES + CHILLING**   *Cook* **17 MINUTES**

2   cups heavy cream

½   cup dried tart cherries, chopped fine

1   cinnamon stick

¼   cup sugar

4   large egg yolks

Salt

Dash of ground cinnamon

Drunken Cherries (see recipe), optional

Elegant is the perfect word to describe this rich and wonderful custard sauce. Spoon it over a cherry pie from the farmer's market or some apple turnovers from the corner bakery. Another day, drizzle it over rich chocolate ice cream and top with strawberries—divine!

LET'S BEGIN Warm the heavy cream, cherries, and cinnamon stick in a medium saucepan for about 15 minutes, using enough heat to allow small bubbles to form at the edges of the cream without bringing to a boil. Stir occasionally.

BUBBLE IT UP Meanwhile, gently whisk together the sugar and egg yolks. Temper the egg mixture with a little hot cream to avoid curdling, then gently mix the egg mixture into the cream mixture. Continue to heat without boiling for 2 to 5 minutes, or until the mixture is thick enough to coat the back of a spoon; stir occasionally. Stir in a pinch of salt and ground cinnamon.

STRAIN & SERVE Strain the sauce into a bowl, using a food mill or Chinois. Press the cherry pieces to release their juice. Let cool. Refrigerate 6 to 8 hours, or overnight to intensify the flavors.

DRUNKEN CHERRIES

Combine 2 pounds (about 6 cups) dried tart cherries in 1½ quarts of port, cognac, or vodka in an airtight container. Set aside 1 to 3 days, or until cherries are plump. Refrigeration is not necessary, but if refrigerated, allow longer for cherries.

> *Makes 8 servings*
> *Per serving: 470 calories, 8g protein, 54g carbohydrates, 23g fat, 15g saturated fat, 55mg cholesterol, 83mg sodium*

CREAMY RASPBERRY CRÈME PIE

Prep **15 MINUTES + CHILLING**

2   packages (8 ounces each) cream cheese, softened

1   package (4-serving size) lemon flavor instant pudding & pie filling

1   cup cold milk

2   teaspoons grated lemon peel

2   cups thawed whipped topping

½   cup raspberry preserves, divided

1   package (6 ounces) graham cracker piecrust

A prepared graham cracker crust, lemon instant pudding, and raspberry preserves turn into a delicious, easy dessert. Try strawberry, blueberry, or red currant preserves instead of raspberry.

LET'S BEGIN Beat the cream cheese, pudding mix, milk, and lemon peel in a large bowl with a wire whisk until well blended. Stir in 1 cup of the whipped topping.

LAYER IT Spread ¼ cup of the preserves over the bottom of the piecrust. Cover the preserves with the pudding mixture. Top with the remaining ¼ cup preserves and remaining 1 cup whipped topping.

CHILL & SLICE Refrigerate the pie for 4 hours before serving. Cover any leftover pie and refrigerate.

Makes 8 servings

Per serving: 473 calories, 6g protein, 46g carbohydrates, 29g fat, 17g saturated fat, 65mg cholesterol, 432mg sodium

Cooking Basics

3 FREEZER CAKE CREATIONS

Ice cream cakes are easy to make. Just be sure to freeze each layer until firm before adding the next one.

BANANA SPLIT CAKE Place slices of pound cake in the bottom of a 9-inch springform pan, cutting to fit as needed. Top with 1 pint chocolate ice cream. Cover with a layer of fudge sauce. Spread 1 pint vanilla ice cream over and top with thinly sliced banana. Top with 1 pint strawberry ice cream and top with thinly sliced strawberries. Freeze for at least 3 hours. Top with whipped cream and sprinkle with chopped walnuts and maraschino cherries.

TRIPLE CHOCOLATE TREAT CAKE Mix 1½ cups chocolate wafer cookie crumbs with 4 tablespoons melted butter in a 9-inch springform pan, then press into the bottom. Spread 1 pint chocolate ice cream over the crumbs. Top with a layer of Nutella (hazelnut-chocolate spread). Spread 1 pint coffee ice cream on top. Spread another layer of Nutella over the ice cream. Top with 1 pint chocolate ice cream and freeze for at least 3 hours. Garnish with whipped cream, chopped toasted hazelnuts, and chocolate shavings.

TROPICAL ISLAND CAKE Toss 2 cups shredded sweetened coconut with 4 tablespoons melted butter. Press on the bottom and sides of a 9-inch pie plate. Spread 1 pint mango or passion fruit sorbet over the coconut crust. Top with 1 pint coconut sorbet. Freeze for at least 3 hours. Garnish with toasted coconut, fresh raspberries, and mint sprigs.

SuperQuick

CREAMY RICE PUDDING

Prep **5 MINUTES**   *Cook* **20 MINUTES**

We love to eat rice pudding for breakfast. It's nutritious and so delicious. Here, the addition of raisins or dried cranberries adds a sparkle of color. If you like, sprinkle some granola on top for extra crunch.

1⅓	cups water
⅔	cup long-grain white rice
1	can (12 ounces) evaporated milk
½	cup raisins, dried cranberries, and/or dried cherries
½	cup granulated sugar
1½	teaspoons vanilla extract
½	teaspoon ground nutmeg
¼	teaspoon salt
2	large eggs, lightly beaten

LET'S BEGIN Bring water and rice to a boil in a medium saucepan. Reduce the heat to low; cover. Cook for 12 to 15 minutes or until liquid is absorbed.

STIR & SERVE Stir in evaporated milk, raisins, sugar, vanilla extract, nutmeg, and salt; bring to a boil. Stir a portion of rice mixture into the eggs. Add egg mixture to rice mixture; mix well with wire whisk. Bring to a boil. Cook, stirring constantly, for 2 minutes. Serve warm or chilled.

> **Makes 6 servings**
> *Per serving: 277 calories, 5g protein, 44g carbohydrates, 6g fat, 4g saturated fat, 76mg cholesterol, 140mg sodium*

COCONUT RICE PUDDING

Substitute ½ cup toasted or untoasted flaked coconut for raisins.

CHOCOLATE PÂTÉ WITH CRANBERRY COULIS

Prep **20 MINUTES**   *Cook* **1 MINUTE + CHILLING**

1½ cups jellied cranberry sauce

¾ cup cranberry juice cocktail

1 teaspoon lime juice

1½ cups whipping cream

1 large egg yolk, beaten slightly

1 package (12 ounces) semisweet chocolate morsels

⅓ cup light or dark corn syrup

¼ cup butter or margarine

1 teaspoon vanilla extract

Whipped cream, for garnish (optional)

Chocolate pâté is heaven on earth. It is like the most delicious and richest flourless chocolate cake you can imagine—serve it in small slices, please! The fresh cranberry coulis (just a fancy word for an uncooked sauce) adds just the right amount of fresh fruity taste.

LET'S BEGIN Line an 8½ × 4½ × 2½-inch loaf pan with plastic wrap. To prepare the coulis, puree the cranberry sauce, cranberry juice, and lime juice in a blender or food processor until smooth. Refrigerate for 1 hour.

STIR & COOL Combine ¼ cup cream with the egg yolk and set aside. Combine the chocolate, corn syrup, and butter in a medium saucepan. Stir over low heat until the chocolate and butter melt. Remove from the heat and stir in the egg mixture. Cook 1 minute over medium heat, stirring constantly. Let cool to room temperature. Beat the remaining 1¼ cups cream and vanilla in a small bowl until soft peaks form. Use a rubber scraper to gently fold the chocolate mixture into the whipped cream. Pour into the prepared pan. Cover with plastic wrap. Refrigerate overnight or freeze 3 hours.

FINAL TOUCH Remove the loaf from the pan and peel away the plastic wrap. Slice into 10 servings. Spoon ¼ cup of the cranberry coulis onto each dessert plate. Place a slice of chocolate pâté in the middle of the coulis. Garnish with whipped cream, if desired.

Makes 10 servings
Per serving: 443 calories, 3g protein, 48g carbohydrates, 30g fat, 18g saturated fat, 86mg cholesterol, 83mg sodium

CHEWY CHOCOLATE NO-BAKE COOKIES

Prep **5 MINUTES**   *Cook* **20 MINUTES + CHILLING**

1   cup (6 ounces) semi-sweet chocolate morsels

5   tablespoons butter or margarine

16   large marshmallows

1   teaspoon vanilla extract

2   cups oat cereal (quick or old fashioned, uncooked)

1   cup raisins, diced dried fruit, shredded coconut, nuts, marshmallows (any combination of these)

These no-bake cookies have it all: crunch (from oat cereal), lots of chocolate taste (thanks to melted chocolate chips), and oodles of fruitiness (from your choice of raisins or dried fruit). You might want to stir up a double batch; we guarantee they'll disappear.

LET'S BEGIN Line baking sheets with waxed paper.

MELT & MIX Melt morsels, butter, and large marshmallows in a large saucepan over low heat, stirring until smooth. Remove from heat; cool slightly. Stir in vanilla extract. Stir in oats and remaining ingredients.

STOP, DROP & SERVE Drop by rounded teaspoonfuls onto prepared sheets. Cover and refrigerate for 2 to 3 hours. Let stand at room temperature about 15 minutes before serving. Store tightly covered in refrigerator.

Makes 3 dozen cookies

Per cookie: 78 calories, 1g protein, 12g carbohydrates, 3g fat, 2g saturated fat, 4mg cholesterol, 15mg sodium

Cooking Basics

RING OF HEARTS

"Present" your desserts just like they do in the finest restaurants using fresh or frozen strawberries or raspberries. Process them to a purée, strain through a sieve to remove the seeds, then sweeten to taste with superfine sugar. Spread enough purée on dessert plates to create a thin, even layer.

To create our Ring of Hearts:

Fill a small plastic squirt bottle (available in cookware stores) with

a fruit puree of contrasting color (or use yogurt, lemon curd, or melted white chocolate). Squirt small dots in a circle about 1 inch from the edge.

Create a ring of hearts by pulling a toothpick (or tip of a small knife) through the center of each dot, creating a heart. Continue around the circle.

CRANBERRY FUDGE

Prep **10 MINUTES**   *Cook* **4 MINUTES + CHILLING**

1   package (12 ounces) semisweet chocolate morsels

¼   cup light or dark corn syrup

½   cup confectioners' sugar

¼   cup evaporated milk

1   teaspoon vanilla extract

1   package (6 ounces) sweetened dried cranberries, any flavor

⅓   cup chopped walnuts or pecans (optional)

This is the ideal fudge for the holidays. Bright red dried cranberries and chopped nuts add a festive touch to this chocolate fudge.

LET'S BEGIN Line an 8-inch square pan with plastic wrap. Set aside.

BLEND & CHILL Combine the chocolate and corn syrup in a medium saucepan. Stir over low heat for 3 to 4 minutes or until the chocolate is melted and mixture is smooth. Remove from the heat. Add the confectioners' sugar, evaporated milk, and vanilla. Stir vigorously with a wooden spoon until the mixture is thick and glossy. Add the cranberries and nuts and mix well. Pour into the prepared pan. Cover and chill until firm, about 2 hours.

CUT & SERVE Turn the fudge out of the pan. Remove the plastic wrap. Cut the fudge into 1½-inch squares. Store covered in the refrigerator. Serve cold or at room temperature.

Makes 25 pieces

Per piece: 109 calories, 2g protein, 19g carbohydrates, 5g fat, 2g saturated fat, 0mg cholesterol, 7mg sodium

CHEWY CARAMEL BARS

Prep **5 MINUTES**   *Microwave* **2 MINUTES + CHILLING**

8   cups sweetened puffed wheat cereal

1   cup salted peanuts

1   package (14 ounces) caramels

2   tablespoons water

We find that the easiest way to cut these treats into bars is with a long, thin knife that has been lightly sprayed with nonstick cooking spray. You may need to wipe the blade between cuts to keep the servings neat.

MIX & MICROWAVE Mix cereal and peanuts in a large bowl. Microwave caramels and water in medium microwaveable bowl on High for 2 minutes or until caramels are melted, stirring every minute. Pour immediately over cereal mixture; mix lightly until well coated.

PRESS & CHILL Press mixture firmly with lightly greased hands into greased 13 × 9-inch pan. Refrigerate until firm. Cut into 24 bars. Store in tightly covered container.

Makes 24 bars

Per bar: 150 calories, 3g protein, 25g carbohydrates, 5g fat, 1g saturated fat, 0mg cholesterol, 95mg sodium

SuperQuick
MANDARIN ORANGE CHOCOLATE FONDUE

Prep **10 MINUTES + MICROWAVING**

¾ cup semisweet chocolate morsels

¼ cup fresh mandarin orange juice

½ tablespoon finely grated mandarin orange peel

2 to 3 cups of the following: orange sections, grapefruit sections, whole strawberries, kiwifruit slices, pear slices, dried apricots

Use fresh clementines or tangerines for this easy dessert. They are available from November to June in most markets.

LET'S BEGIN Combine the first 3 ingredients in a small microwaveable bowl. Microwave on High for 30 seconds. Stir with a wire whisk until the juice is incorporated and chocolate is smooth.

HEAT & DIP Serve in a fondue pot over a very low flame. Use long fondue forks to spear and dip the fruit.

Makes 4 servings

Per serving: 143 calories, 1g protein, 20g carbohydrates, 9g fat, 5g saturated fat, 0mg cholesterol, 3mg sodium

NO CRUST PUMPKIN PIE

Prep **10 MINUTES**   *Cook* **5 MINUTES + CHILLING**

2 tablespoons water

2 envelopes (.25 ounce each) unflavored gelatin

2¼ cups evaporated low-fat milk

1 can (15 ounces) pure pumpkin (not pumpkin pie mix)

½ cup packed dark brown sugar or low-calorie sweetener equivalent

2 teaspoons pumpkin pie spice

1 teaspoon vanilla extract

When you think about it, a pumpkin pie is a spiced pumpkin custard that is baked in a pie shell. Here you can enjoy all the flavor of a delicious pumpkin custard without the added calories of the crust. Good idea!

LET'S BEGIN Coat a 9-inch deep-dish pie plate with nonstick cooking spray.

FIX IT UP Sprinkle gelatin over water in a medium bowl. Let stand for 5 to 10 minutes or until softened. Mixture may be firm. Bring 1 cup evaporated milk just to a boil in small saucepan. Slowly stir hot evaporated milk into gelatin. Stir in remaining evaporated milk, pumpkin, sugar, pumpkin pie spice, and vanilla extract.

SERVE IT UP Pour mixture into pie plate. Refrigerate for 2 hours or until set.

Makes 8 servings

Per serving: 140 calories, 4g protein, 19g carbohydrates, 1g fat, 1g saturated fat, 3mg cholesterol, 31mg sodium

BAKE NOT BROWNIE BARS

Prep **20 MINUTES**   *Cook* **15 MINUTES + CHILLING**

38   squares graham
     crackers, finely crushed
     (about 2½ cups crumbs)

2   cups miniature
     marshmallows

1   cup walnuts, chopped

1   package (6 ounces)
     semisweet chocolate
     morsels

1   cup evaporated milk

½   cup light corn syrup

¼   teaspoon salt

1   tablespoon butter or
     margarine

1   tablespoon vanilla
     extract

These brownies are wonderbars. No baking, yet they look, taste, and feel exactly like the real thing!

LET'S BEGIN Mix the crumbs, marshmallows, and nuts in a large bowl and set aside. Stir the chocolate, milk, corn syrup, and salt in a large saucepan over low heat until the chocolate is melted.

BUBBLE & BOIL Increase the heat to medium and bring to a full boil, stirring constantly. Boil for 10 minutes, stirring constantly. Remove from the heat and stir in the butter and vanilla.

STIR & CHILL Immediately stir the chocolate mixture into crumb mixture. Press into a greased 9-inch square baking pan. Refrigerate until set, about 3 hours. Cut into thirty-six 1½-inch squares.

Makes 36 squares

Per square: 100 calories, 1g protein, 13g carbohydrates, 5g fat, 1g saturated fat, 2mg cholesterol, 62mg sodium

---

Food Facts

CHARLOTTES, TRIFLES, AND FOOLS

Do you know the difference between these three festive desserts?

A charlotte is a molded dessert, made in a pail-shaped mold that is lined with ladyfingers, sponge cake, or buttered bread. The mold is filled with layers or a mixture of fruit and custard or whipped cream. The dessert is chilled, unmolded, and garnished.

A trifle is a classic English Christmas dessert. It consists of sponge cake or ladyfingers that are moistened with liqueur or sherry and used to line an elegant pedestal glass bowl. The center is filled with jam and custard and the top decorated with piped whipped cream. Toasted nuts, fruits, or grated chocolate often serve as its decoration.

A fruit fool is also an English dessert. This casual dessert is made of cold pureed fruit and stiffly whipped cream that is gently folded together and swirled decoratively, so the colors remain distinct.

SuperQuick
CHOCOLATE S'MORES FONDUE

Prep **10 MINUTES** *Cook* **5 MINUTES**

½ cup milk

1 package (11 ounces) peanut butter and milk chocolate morsels

1 jar (7 ounces) marshmallow cream

1 cup graham cracker crumbs

8 Granny Smith apples, cored and sliced

Our fondue is guaranteed to bring out the kid in any adult. All the fun taste of s'mores is packed into a smooth and chocolaty fondue sauce. To keep the apple slices from browning, toss them in a little bit of fresh lemon juice.

LET'S BEGIN Heat the milk in a medium, heavy-bottomed saucepan over medium-high heat just until hot (do not boil). Reduce the heat to low. Add the morsels and stir until mixture is smooth. Add the marshmallow cream and whisk until smooth. Remove from the heat.

SERVE IT UP Transfer the mixture to a fondue pot or a serving bowl. Place the graham cracker crumbs in a separate serving bowl. To serve, dip the apple slices into the warm chocolate mixture and then dip into the graham cracker crumbs.

Makes 6 servings

Per serving: 545 calories, 5g protein, 97g carbohydrates, 18g fat, 10g saturated fat, 11mg cholesterol, 108mg sodium

JUST-PLAIN-CHOCOLATE FONDUE

You can substitute an 11.5-ounce package of milk chocolate morsels or a 12-ounce package of semisweet chocolate morsels for the peanut butter & milk chocolate morsels.

EASY CINNAMON FUDGE

Prep **20 MINUTES** *Cook* **2 MINUTES + CHILLING**

3¾ cups (1 pound)
    confectioners' sugar

½ cup unsweetened cocoa

¼ to ½ teaspoon cinnamon

½ cup butter

¼ cup milk

1½ teaspoons vanilla extract

1 cup chopped nuts

These no-bake cookies have it all: crunch (from oat cereal), lots of chocolate taste (thanks to melted chocolate chips), and oodles of fruitiness (from your choice of raisins or dried fruit).

LET'S BEGIN Mix together the sugar, cocoa, and cinnamon in a medium bowl. Heat the butter and milk in a small saucepan until butter melts. Remove from heat and stir in the vanilla. Pour the hot milk and butter into the sugar mixture. Stir in the nuts. Line an 8-inch square baking pan with foil, allowing the foil to extend over the sides. Butter the foil. Pour the fudge into the prepared pan. Refrigerate at least 1 hour.

FINAL TOUCH Use foil to lift the fudge out of the pan. Peel off the foil. Cut the fudge into 2-inch squares, then cut each square in half diagonally, making triangles.

Makes 32 pieces

Per piece: 117 calories, 1g protein, 15g carbohydrates, 6g fat, 2g saturated fat, 8mg cholesterol, 33mg sodium

---

Cook to Cook

WHAT KIND OF WAFFLE IRON IS BEST?

"*Waffle irons are not created equal.* You have choices—electric or stovetop. While the stovetop model may conjure up the fantasy of a hearty breakfast in a country farmhouse, the electric version is a far better choice.

Electric waffle irons have a nonstick surface, which gives years of use without ever having to season the iron as you do for a stovetop model. The nonstick surface also makes clean-up a trouble-free task.

With an electric waffle iron, the heat is regulated by a thermostat, *which creates constant, even heat to produce crisp, golden waffles every time.* Adjusting the heat on your stove for a stovetop model can be frustrating, as you are sure to either burn or undercook the first waffle in every batch. Electric irons cook the top and bottom of the waffle at the same time—no turning needed, as with the stovetop model.

Check out the thickness of the grids: the traditional electric models have *shallow grids that make thin waffles and Belgian waffle irons have deep grids that make thicker waffles* (about 1¼ inches thick). The choice is yours!"

SuperQuick
NUTTY PUMPKIN WAFFLES

Prep **10 MINUTES**   *Cook* **16 MINUTES**

2	cups all-purpose flour
¼	cup sugar
1	tablespoon cornstarch
2	teaspoons baking powder
2	teaspoons ground cinnamon
½	teaspoon salt
¼	teaspoon ground ginger
¼	teaspoon ground nutmeg
2	large eggs, separated
1¾	cups milk
½	cup canned pumpkin
2	tablespoons butter or margarine, melted
¾	cup chopped nuts

Pumpkin Maple Sauce (see recipe)

Serve these on a brisk fall morning to fuel the family for a hike in the woods or a morning of leaf-raking. You'll have no trouble getting them on their way with these tempting treats.

LET'S BEGIN Preheat the waffle iron. Combine the first 8 ingredients in a large bowl and stir to mix well. Combine the egg yolks, milk, and pumpkin in a medium bowl, stir to mix well and add to the flour mixture. Stir in the butter. Place the egg whites in a medium bowl and beat at high speed with an electric mixer until stiff peaks form. Gently fold the egg whites into the pumpkin mixture.

BROWN & SERVE Depending on the size of your waffle iron, pour ½ cup to 1½ cups batter onto the hot iron and sprinkle with about 1½ tablespoons of the nuts. Close the lid and cook for 1 to 2 minutes or until the waffle is browned and the steaming stops.* Repeat with the remaining batter and nuts. Serve immediately with the Pumpkin Maple Sauce.

*Amounts of batter and cooking times vary for different waffle irons. Check the manufacturer's directions for your model for specific recommendations.

PUMPKIN MAPLE SAUCE

To make this sauce, stir together 1 cup maple syrup, ¾ cup canned pumpkin, and ¼ teaspoon ground cinnamon in small saucepan. Cook over medium heat until warm.

Makes 8 servings

Per serving: 412 calories, 9g protein, 65g carbohydrates, 14g fat, 4g saturated fat, 66mg cholesterol, 274mg sodium

SuperQuick
VERY BERRY FRENCH TOAST

Prep **15 MINUTES**   *Cook* **15 MINUTES**

4   large eggs

½   cup evaporated milk

2   tablespoons butter or margarine, melted

1   tablespoon sugar

¼   teaspoon ground cinnamon

¼   teaspoon vanilla extract

Dash of salt

1   French bread loaf

Cinnamon Vanilla Sauce or Maple Berry Sauce (see recipes)

2   cups fresh berries (strawberries, blueberries, or blackberries, or a combination)

Confectioners' sugar, vanilla ice cream, or whipped cream (optional)

This divine French toast is special enough for a family celebration or a casual brunch. It's a showcase for gorgeous summer berries—make it when they're at their peak.

LET'S BEGIN Whisk together the eggs, milk, butter, sugar, cinnamon, vanilla, and salt in a medium bowl. Cut 8 1-inch thick slices of bread on the diagonal from the bread loaf. Place the bread in a single layer in a large shallow dish. Pour the egg mixture over the bread and turn to coat it evenly. Let the bread stand for 2 minutes.

COOK QUICKLY Melt the butter in a large nonstick skillet over medium heat. Place 4 slices of the bread in the skillet and cook for 2 minutes on each side, or until golden. Repeat with the remaining bread.

TOP & SERVE To serve, place two slices of the French toast on each of 4 plates. Arrange the berries on top and spoon the Cinnamon Vanilla Sauce or the Maple Berry Sauce over the toast. Garnish with confectioners' sugar, ice cream, or whipped cream, if you wish.

CINNAMON VANILLA SAUCE

To make this sauce, combine 1 cup evaporated milk, 3 tablespoons sugar, 2 teaspoons cornstarch, and 2 cinnamon sticks in medium saucepan. Cook over medium heat, stirring constantly, until the mixture comes to a boil and thickens slightly. Remove from the heat and stir in the vanilla. Remove the cinnamon sticks.

MAPLE BERRY SAUCE

Combine 1 tablespoon pure maple syrup, 1 tablespoon sugar, and 2 cups strawberries, blueberries, or blackberries (or a combination) in a small saucepan and cook over low heat, stirring often, until the berries begin to soften and release their juices. Serve over French toast.

Makes 4 servings

Per serving: 455 calories, 13g protein, 48g carbohydrates, 19g fat, 10g saturated fat, 235mg cholesterol, 472mg sodium

ORANGE DESSERT CREPES

Prep **20 MINUTES + CHILLING AND FREEZING**

3   tablespoons orange marmalade

3   tablespoons orange flavored liqueur or 2 teaspoons orange extract

3   oranges, peeled, cut into quarter-cartwheel slices

1   quart vanilla ice cream, slightly softened

2   tablespoons grated orange peel

10   ready-to-use crepes or prepared crepes

¼   cup toasted sliced almonds

Fresh mint leaves, if desired

What's the next new thing? Crepes, because they're so easy and elegant and they fit the way we eat today . . . light, pretty, and with plenty of do-ahead steps.

LET'S BEGIN In a large bowl, stir together the marmalade and orange liqueur or extract. Add the orange slices and toss gently. Chill for 30 minutes. In another large bowl, mix the ice cream with the orange peel. Freeze for 30 minutes or until firm.

FILL & FREEZE Lay each crepe on a flat work surface with the brown side down. Spoon about 3 heaping tablespoons of ice cream along the center of each, then fold in the ends and roll up. Place the filled crepe on a tray or pan in the freezer as each is completed. Freeze for 1 to 2 hours or until firm.

FINAL TOUCH To serve, place 2 crepes on an individual dessert plate. Spoon some of the orange sauce over each serving. Sprinkle with almonds and garnish with fresh mint, if desired.

Makes 5 servings

Per serving: 637 calories, 17g protein, 75g carbohydrates, 30g fat, 12g saturated fat, 252mg cholesterol, 460mg sodium

---

Cooking Basics

CREPE MAKING—1, 2, 3!

1. Whisk It When making crepes, you need a batter that's smooth and free of lumps. Whisk vigorously when mixing the batter.

2. Spread It Use a 6- to 8-inch crepe pan or a nonstick skillet and heat the pan over medium heat until it's hot. Add 3 to 4 tablespoons of batter to the pan.

Immediately lift the pan and tilt it in a rotating motion to spread the batter over the bottom of the pan in a very thin layer.

3. Cook It When the bottom side is done, the batter will start to bubble—it'll only take about 45 seconds. Lift the crepe using a spatula to make sure the underside is

golden brown before flipping it over. Cook the second side until it is golden—about 15 to 20 seconds. Stack the cooked crepes with waxed paper layered between them to keep them from sticking together. Fill with your favorite filling and enjoy!

SuperQuick
RICE CREPES
Prep **15 MINUTES**   *Cook* **10 MINUTES**

1   carton (8 ounces) egg substitute

⅔   cup evaporated skim milk

1   tablespoon margarine, melted

½   cup all-purpose flour

1   tablespoon sugar

1   cup cooked rice

Vegetable cooking spray

2½ cups fresh fruit (strawberries, raspberries, blueberries, or other favorite fruit)

Low-sugar fruit spread (optional)

Light sour cream (optional)

1   tablespoon confectioner's sugar for garnish (optional)

LET'S BEGIN Combine the egg substitute, milk, and margarine in a medium bowl. Stir in the flour and sugar until smooth and well blended. Stir in the rice and let stand for 5 minutes.

COOK QUICKLY Heat an 8-inch nonstick skillet or crepe pan over medium heat for 3 minutes, then coat with cooking spray. Spoon ¼ cup of the batter into the pan. Lift the pan off the heat and quickly tilt the pan in a rotating motion so the bottom of the pan is completely covered with batter. Place the pan back on the heat and continue cooking until the surface is dry, about 45 seconds. Turn the crepe over and cook for 15 to 20 seconds. Set aside. Continue with the remaining crepe batter until you have 10 crepes. Stack the crepes with waxed paper between each one.

TOP & SERVE Fill each crepe with your favorite fruit, then the fruit spread, or sour cream. Roll up the crepes and sprinkle with confectioner's sugar, if desired. Serve warm or at room temperature.

Makes 10 crepes

Per crepe: 100 calories, 5g protein, 17g carbohydrates, 1g fat, 0g saturated fat, 1mg cholesterol, 137mg sodium

TRIPLE LAYER EGGNOG PIE

Prep **10 MINUTES**   *Microwave* **1 MINUTE + CHILLING**

10	caramels
1	cup cold milk
1	package (6 ounces) graham cracker piecrust
½	cup chopped pecans, toasted
1	cup cold eggnog
2	packages (4-serving size each) vanilla flavor instant pudding & pie filling
2	cups thawed whipped topping

During the holiday season it is easy to purchase ready-made eggnog in cartons in the dairy case. And nothing says holiday quite as much as eggnog. This delicious pie makes 10 generous servings.

LET'S BEGIN Combine the caramels with 1 tablespoon milk in a medium microwavable bowl. Microwave on Medium (50%) for 30 seconds, stirring until the caramels are completely melted. Pour into the crust and sprinkle the top with pecans.

BLEND & LAYER Stir the remaining milk and eggnog in a large bowl. Add the pudding mix and beat with a wire whisk for 2 minutes or until thick. Spoon 1½ cups into the crust. Stir 1 cup of the whipped topping into the remaining pudding and spread over the pie. Top with the remaining 1 cup whipped topping.

CHILL & SLICE Refrigerate the pie for at least 3 hours before serving. Cover and refrigerate leftover pie.

Makes 10 servings

Per serving: 340 calories, 3g protein, 47g carbohydrates, 16g fat, 7g saturated fat, 15mg cholesterol, 420mg sodium

TIRAMISU

Prep **30 MINUTES + CHILLING**   *Cook* **7 MINUTES**

4   egg yolks

⅔   cup sugar

½   cup milk

8   ounces mascarpone cheese

1   tablespoon sweet Marsala or 1 tablespoon rum or ⅛ teaspoon rum extract + 1 tablespoon water

1   cup whipping cream

½   teaspoon vanilla extract

18   ladyfingers

1   cup strong brewed coffee or espresso, cooled

1½   teaspoons unsweetened cocoa

Translated from Italian, tiramisu means "to carry me up." Many folks think it means "carry me to heaven." This recipe is so dreamy that your guests won't be able to stop with just one piece. It uses mascarpone, a double-rich, double-cream cheese from the Lombardy region in Italy with a wonderful delicate flavor. The whole dessert is then flavored with coffee, Marsala, and a hint of brandy.

LET'S BEGIN Whisk the egg yolks in a small saucepan until well combined. Gradually whisk in the sugar, then whisk in the milk. Place the mixture over medium heat and cook, stirring constantly until it boils, about 6 minutes. Boil for 1 minute, stirring constantly. Remove from the heat and transfer to a medium bowl. Place plastic wrap directly on top of the mixture to prevent a film from forming. Refrigerate for 1 hour until cooled.

MIX IT UP Add the mascarpone to the cooled mixture and stir until well blended. Stir in the wine and set the cheese mixture aside. Beat the cream at high speed with an electric mixer until stiff peaks form. Beat in the vanilla. Fold half of the cream mixture into the cheese mixture.

MIX IT UP Separate the ladyfingers into halves and brush both sides of each one with the coffee. Place half of the ladyfingers in the bottom of an 8-inch square glass baking dish. Spread half of the cheese mixture over the ladyfingers. Top with the remaining ladyfingers and cover with the remaining cheese mixture. Top with the reserved whipped cream and sift the cocoa over the top. Cover and refrigerate for at least 4 hours.

Makes 10 servings
Per serving: 280 calories, 7g protein, 28g carbohydrates, 16g fat, 9g saturated fat, 200mg cholesterol, 69mg sodium

CREDITS

PAGE 2 Cherry Marketing Institute: Photo for Cherry Cinnamon Crème Anglaise courtesy of The Cherry Marketing Institute. Used with permission.

PAGE 8 Land O'Lakes: Photo for Chocolate Lover's Ice Cream Pie courtesy of Land O'Lakes, Inc. Used with permission.

PAGE 16 Kraft Foods: Photo for Dessert Waffles courtesy of Kraft Kitchens. Used with permission.

PAGE 18 B&G Foods: Recipe for Warm Maple Nut Sundaes courtesy of B&G Foods. Used with permission.

PAGE 19 Del Monte: Recipe for Angel Food Ambrosia courtesy of Del Monte Foods. Used with permission.

PAGE 19 Almond Board of California: Recipe for Fast Chocolate-Almond Fudge courtesy of the Almond Board of California. Used with permission.

PAGE 20 Hershey Foods: Recipe for Double-Dip Strawberries courtesy of Hershey Kitchens, Hershey Foods Corporation, Hershey, PA.

PAGE 21 Hershey Foods: Photo and recipe for No Bake Fudge Cookies courtesy of Hershey Kitchens, Hershey Foods Corporation, Hershey, PA.

PAGES 22/23 Ocean Spray Cranberries: Photo and recipe for White Chocolate Clusters courtesy of Ocean Spray Cranberries, Inc. Used with permission.

PAGE 24 Kraft Foods: Recipe for Super Power Crunch Bars courtesy of Kraft Kitchens. Used with permission.

PAGE 25 USA Rice Federation: Recipe for Banana Kiwi Pudding courtesy of the USA Rice Federation. Used with permission.

PAGES 26/27 Nestlé: Photo and recipe for Easy Peanut Butter Chocolate Cheesecake Pie courtesy of Nestlé. Used with permission.

PAGE 28 Nestlé: Recipe for Easy Tiramisu courtesy of Nestlé. Used with permission.

PAGE 29 Hershey Foods: Recipe for Cherry Chocolate Shortcake courtesy of Hershey Kitchens, Hershey Foods Corporation, Hershey, PA. Used with permission.

PAGES 30/31 Kraft Foods: Photo and recipe for Dessert Waffles courtesy of Kraft Kitchens. Used with permission.

PAGE 32 Nestlé: Photo and recipe for Quick Pumpkin Pudding courtesy of Nestlé. Used with permission.

PAGE 33 Ocean Spray Cranberries: Photo and recipe for Chocolate Truffles courtesy of Ocean Spray Cranberries, Inc. Used with permission.

PAGE 34 Land O'Lakes: Photo for Luscious Lemony Fruit "Shortcakes" courtesy of Land O'Lakes, Inc. Used with permission.

PAGE 36 California Strawberry Commission: Recipe for California Fruit Dips courtesy of the © California Strawberry Commission. All rights reserved. Used with permission.

PAGE 37 Wisconsin Milk Marketing Board: Recipe for Sabayon with Fresh Fruits courtesy of the Wisconsin Milk Marketing Board, Inc. Used with permission.

PAGE 38 Wisconsin Milk Marketing Board: Recipe for Grilled Fruit Kabobs with Tropical Yogurt Sauce courtesy of the Wisconsin Milk Marketing Board, Inc. Used with permission.

PAGE 39 McCormick: Recipe for Cinnamony Spiced Peaches courtesy of McCormick. Used with permission.

PAGE 39 McCormick: Recipe for Bananas Foster courtesy of McCormick. Used with permission.

PAGES 40/41 Land O'Lakes: Photo and recipe for Luscious Lemony Fruit "Shortcakes" courtesy of Land O'Lakes, Inc. Used with permission.

PAGE 42 Mott's: Recipe for Apple Split courtesy of Mott's. Used with permission.

PAGE 43 Nestlé: Recipe for Tiny Fruit Tarts courtesy of Nestlé. Used with permission.

PAGE 44 Almond Board of California: Recipe for Honey Almond Cream with Berries courtesy of the Almond Board of California. Used with permission.

PAGE 45 Nestlé: Recipe for Pineapple Pecan Cups courtesy of Nestlé. Used with permission.

PAGES 46/47 Produce for Better Health Foundation: Recipe for Ambrosia courtesy of the Produce for Better Health Foundation. Used with permission.

PAGE 46 B&G Foods: Recipe for Fruit Tacos courtesy of B&G Foods. Used with permission.

PAGE 48 Mott's: Photo and recipe for Kaleidoscope Pops courtesy of Mott's. Used with permission.

PAGE 49 Produce for Better Health Foundation: Photo and recipe for Grapes with Ginger Cream courtesy of the Produce for Better Health Foundation. Used with permission.

PAGE 50 Mott's: Photo and recipe for Fruity Parfaits courtesy of Mott's. Used with permission.

PAGE 51 B&G Foods: Recipe for Raspberry Trifle courtesy of B&G Foods. Used with permission.

PAGE 52 Hershey Foods: Photo for Chocolate Quesadillas courtesy of Hershey Kitchens, Hershey Foods Corporation, Hershey, PA. Used with permission.

PAGE 54/55 Land O'Lakes: Photo and recipe for Snickerdoodle Ice Cream courtesy of Land O'Lakes, Inc. Used with permission.

PAGE 56 Hershey Foods: Photo and recipe for Banana Pops courtesy of Hershey Kitchens, Hershey Foods Corporation, Hershey, PA. Used with permission.

PAGE 57 Hershey Foods: Recipe for Rocky Road Sundae courtesy of Hershey Kitchens, Hershey Foods Corporation, Hershey, PA. Used with permission.

PAGES 58/59 Ocean Spray Cranberries: Photo and recipe for Polka Dot Popcorn Balls courtesy of Ocean Spray Cranberries, Inc. Used with permission.

PAGE 60 Hershey Foods: Photo and recipe for Lunch Box Peanut Butter Treats courtesy of Hershey Kitchens, Hershey Foods Corporation, Hershey, PA. Used with permission.

PAGE 61 Hershey Foods: Recipe for Snacking Blocks courtesy of Hershey Kitchens, Hershey Foods Corporation, Hershey, PA. Used with permission.

PAGE 62 M&M/Mars: Recipe for Wake 'em Up Wacky Waffles courtesy of M&M/Mars. Used with permission.

PAGE 63 M&M/Mars: Recipe for Tiny Love Cakes courtesy of M&M/Mars. Used with permission.

PAGES 64/65 Hershey Foods: Photo and recipe for Chocolate Quesadillas courtesy of Hershey Kitchens, Hershey Foods Corporation, Hershey, PA. Used with permission.

PAGE 66 Land O'Lakes: Recipe for Microwave Peanut Butter Fudge courtesy of Land O'Lakes, Inc. Used with permission.

PAGE 67 Hershey Foods: Recipe for Chocolate Nuggets Critters courtesy of Hershey Kitchens, Hershey Foods Corporation, Hershey, PA. Used with permission.

PAGES 68/69 Land O'Lakes: Photo and recipe for "Make Mine Chocolate" Waffles courtesy of Land O'Lakes, Inc. Used with permission.

PAGE 70 Almond Board of California: Recipe for Tortillas Fantasticas courtesy of the Almond Board of California. Used with permission.

PAGE 71 Hershey Foods: Recipe for Butterscotch Fudge Cut-Outs courtesy of Hershey Kitchens, Hershey Foods Corporation, Hershey, PA. Used with permission.

PAGE 71 Nestlé: Recipe for Dirt Cake courtesy of Nestlé. Used with permission.

PAGE 72 Kraft Foods: Recipe for Peanut Butter S'mores courtesy of Kraft Kitchens. Used with permission.

PAGE 73 M&M/Mars: Recipe for Circus Pie courtesy of M&M/Mars. Used with permission.

PAGE 74 Kraft Foods: Photo for Coconut Fudge Bars courtesy of Kraft Kitchens. Used with permission.

PAGE 76 Nestlé: Recipe for Strawberry Chiffon Pie courtesy of Nestlé. Used with permission.

PAGE 77 California Strawberry Commission: Recipe for Strawberry-Chocolate Mousse Parfait courtesy of the © California Strawberry Commission. All rights reserved. Used with permission.

PAGE 78 Kraft Foods: Recipe for Coconut Fudge Bars courtesy of Kraft Kitchens. Used with permission.

PAGE 79 Wisconsin Milk Marketing Board: Recipe for Butterscotch Cream Pudding courtesy of the Wisconsin Milk Marketing Board, Inc. Used with permission.

PAGES 80/81 Hershey Foods: Photo and recipe for Cool 'n' Creamy Chocolate Pie courtesy of Hershey Kitchens, Hershey Foods Corporation, Hershey, PA. Used with permission.

PAGE 82 Wisconsin Milk Marketing Board: Recipe for Chilled Orange Soufflé courtesy of the Wisconsin Milk Marketing Board, Inc. Used with permission.

PAGE 83 McCormick: Recipe for Root Beer Float Pops courtesy of McCormick. Used with permission.

PAGE 83 USA Rice Federation: Recipe for Vanilla Custard Freeze courtesy of the USA Rice Federation. Used with permission.

PAGE 84 Hershey Foods: Photo and recipe for Chocolate Mallow Swirl Pie courtesy of Hershey Kitchens, Hershey Foods Corporation, Hershey, PA. Used with permission.

PAGE 85 Kraft Foods: Recipe for Chewy Chocolate Cherry Squares courtesy of Kraft Kitchens. Used with permission.

PAGE 86 Hershey Foods: Photo and recipe for Mini Chocolate Pies courtesy of Hershey Kitchens, Hershey Foods Corporation, Hershey, PA. Used with permission.

PAGE 87 Sunkist: Recipe for Classic Lemon Curd courtesy of Sunkist Growers, Inc. Used with permission.

PAGE 87 McCormick: Recipe for Chocolate Mousse courtesy of McCormick.

PAGES 88/89 Ocean Spray Cranberries: Photo and recipe for Cranberry & White Chocolate Parfaits courtesy of Ocean Spray Cranberries, Inc. Used with permission.

PAGE 90 Nestlé: Photo and recipe for Florida Key Lime Pie courtesy of Nestlé. Used with permission.

PAGE 91 California Strawberry Commission: Recipe for Strawberry-Lemon Parfait courtesy of the © California Strawberry Commission. All rights reserved. Used with permission.

PAGE 92 California Strawberry Commission: Photo and recipe for Strawberry Tiramisu courtesy of the © California Strawberry Commission. All rights reserved. Used with permission.

PAGE 93 Ocean Spray Cranberries: Photo and recipe for Fruity Mocha Mousse courtesy of the © California Strawberry Commission. All rights reserved. Used with permission.

PAGE 94 Nestlé: Photo for Easy Pumpkin Ice Cream courtesy of Nestlé. Used with permission.

PAGE 96 California Strawberry Commission: Recipe for Berry Blender Ice Cream courtesy of the © California Strawberry Commission. All rights reserved. Used with permission.

PAGE 97 Del Monte: Recipe for Simple Peach Sorbet courtesy of Del Monte Foods. Used with permission.

PAGE 98 Del Monte: Recipe for Tropi-nana Split courtesy of Del Monte Foods. Used with permission.

PAGE 98 Oceanspray: Recipe for Tropical Pink Sorbet courtesy of Ocean Spray Cranberries, Inc. Used with permission.

PAGE 99 Wisconsin Milk Marketing Board: Recipe for Banana Splits courtesy of the Wisconsin Milk Marketing Board, Inc. Used with permission.

PAGES 100/101 Land O'Lakes: Photo and recipe for Chocolate Lover's Ice Cream Pie courtesy of Land O'Lakes, Inc. Used with permission.

PAGE 102 Sunkist: Recipe for Citrus Yogurt Sundaes courtesy of Sunkist Growers, Inc. Used with permission.

PAGE 103 Almond Board of California: Recipe for Almond Mocha Ice Cream courtesy of the Almond Board of California. Used with permission.

PAGE 104 B&G Foods: Recipe for Ice Creamwiches courtesy of B&G Foods. Used with permission.

PAGE 105 Nestlé: Photo and recipe for Blushing Snowballs courtesy of Nestlé. Used with permission.

PAGES 106/107 Nestlé: Photo and recipe for Easy Pumpkin Ice Cream courtesy of Nestlé. Used with permission.

PAGE 108 Ocean Spray Cranberries: Photo and recipe for Cranberry Orange Granita courtesy of Ocean Spray Cranberries, Inc. Used with permission.

PAGE 109 Cherry Marketing Institute: Photo and recipe for Cherry Spumoni courtesy of The Cherry Marketing Institute. Used with permission.

PAGE 110 Nestlé: Photo for Very Berry French Toast courtesy of Nestlé. Used with permission.

PAGE 112 Nestlé: Photo and recipe for Easy & Elegant Cheesecake courtesy of Nestlé. Used with permission.

PAGE 113 Kraft Foods: Recipe for Black-Bottom Mini Cheesecakes courtesy of Kraft Kitchens. Used with permission.

PAGES 114/115 Kraft Foods: Photo recipe for Tropical Cheesecakes courtesy of Kraft Kitchens. Used with permission.

PAGE 116 Cherry Marketing Institute: Photo and recipe for Cherry Cheese Heart courtesy of The Cherry Marketing Institute. Used with permission.

PAGE 117 USA Rice Federation: Recipe for Peppermint Cloud Rice Pie courtesy of the USA Rice Federation. Used with permission.

PAGES 118/119 Cherry Marketing Institute: Photo and recipe for Cherry-Cinnamon Crème Anglaise courtesy of The Cherry Marketing Institute. Used with permission.

PAGE 120 Kraft Foods: Recipe for Creamy Raspberry Crème Pie courtesy of Kraft Kitchens. Used with permission.

PAGE 121 Nestlé: Recipe for Creamy Rice Pudding courtesy of Nestlé. Used with permission.

PAGE 122 Ocean Spray Cranberries: Recipe for Chocolate Pâté with Cranberry Coulis courtesy of Ocean Spray Cranberries, Inc. Used with permission.

PAGE 123 Nestlé: Recipe for Chewy Chocolate No-Bake Cookies courtesy of Nestlé. Used with permission.

PAGES 124/125 Ocean Spray Cranberries: Photo and recipe for Cranberry Fudge courtesy of Ocean Spray Cranberries, Inc. Used with permission.

PAGES 126/127 Kraft Foods: Photo and recipe for Chewy Caramel Bars courtesy of Kraft Kitchens. Used with permission.

PAGE 128 Sunkist: Recipe for Mandarin Orange Chocolate Fondue courtesy of Sunkist Growers, Inc. Used with permission.

PAGE 128 Nestlé: Recipe for No-Crust Pumpkin Pie courtesy of Nestlé. Used with permission.

PAGE 129 Kraft Foods: Recipe for Bake Not Brownie Bars courtesy of Kraft Kitchens. Used with permission.

PAGE 130 Nestlé: Photo and recipe for Chocolate S'mores Fondue courtesy of Nestlé. Used with permission.

PAGE 131 McCormick: Recipe for Easy Cinnamon Fudge courtesy of McCormick. Used with permission.

PAGES 132/133 Nestlé: Photo and recipe for Nutty Pumpkin Waffles courtesy of Nestlé. Used with permission.

PAGES 134/135 Nestlé: Photo and recipe for Very Berry French Toast courtesy of Nestlé. Used with permission.

PAGE 136 Sunkist: Recipe for Orange Dessert Crepes courtesy of Sunkist Growers, Inc. Used with permission.

PAGE 137 USA Rice Federation: Photo and recipe for Rice Crepes courtesy of the USA Rice Federation. Used with permission.

PAGE 138 Kraft Foods: Recipe for Triple Layer Eggnog Pie courtesy of Kraft Kitchens. Used with permission.

PAGE 139 Wisconsin Milk Marketing Board: Recipe for Tiramisu courtesy of the Wisconsin Milk Marketing Boarc, Inc. Used with permission.

RODALE INC.
www.rodale.com

Almond Board of California
www.almondsarein.com

B&G Foods
www.bgfoods.com

California Strawberry Commission
www.calstrawberry.com

Cherry Marketing Institute
www.usacherries.com

Del Monte
www.delmonte.com

Hershey Foods
www.hersheykitchens.com

Kraft Foods
www.kraftfoods.com

Land O'Lakes
www.landolakes.com

McCormick
www.mccormick.com

M&M/Mars
www.marsbrightideas.com

Mott's
www.motts.com

Nestlé
www.Nestle.com

Ocean Spray Cranberries
www.oceanspray.com

Produce for Better Health Foundation
www.5aday.org

Sunkist
www.sunkist.com

USA Rice Federation
www.usarice.com

Wisconsin Milk Marketing Board
www.wisdairy.com

INDEX

✔ Designates a SuperQuick recipe that gets you in and out of the kitchen in 30 minutes or less!
Boldface page numbers refer to photographs. *Italicized* page numbers refer to boxed text.